**Bible biog**
*Series editor*

D0353265

# Abraham

# Abraham
## Believing God
## in an alien world

## David Jackman

Inter-Varsity Press

INTER-VARSITY PRESS
*38 De Montfort Street, Leicester LE1 7GP, England*

*First published 1987*

**British Library Cataloguing in Publication Data**

Jackman, David
   Abraham: believing God in an alien world.——
   (Bible biographies series).
   1. Abraham  2. Faith——Case studies
   I. Title  II. Series
   248.4    BS580.A3

ISBN 0–85110–498–3

Phototypeset in Linotron Times by Input Typesetting Ltd,
London
Printed in Great Britain by Cox & Wyman Ltd, Reading

*Inter-Varsity Press is the publishing division of the
Universities and Colleges Christian Fellowship
(formerly the Inter-Varsity Fellowship), a student
movement linking Christian Unions in universities and
colleges throughout the United Kingdom and the Republic
of Ireland, and a member movement of the International
Fellowship of Evangelical Students. For information
about local and national activities write to UCCF, 38
De Montfort Street, Leicester LE1 7GP.*

# Contents

# General preface

For many Christians today the Old Testament is almost a closed book. There is comparatively little preaching of it from our pulpits, and even less personal study (apart from a few well-loved and well-worn purple passages). In an age when even the familiar stories of the ministry of Jesus, as recorded in the New Testament gospels, are increasingly unknown among children and young people generally, it is not surprising that many of these same people hardly know where to begin when they come to know Christ personally and are told to read the whole Bible.

This series is an attempt to meet that need, at a level that young Christians can readily understand and in a way with which they will be able easily to identify. It seeks to present an attractive way in particularly to the Old Testament and its riches, because it starts where we all are – with the everyday life experience of real people. By mining the rich veins of biography and true story, we hope to set the Bible characters in their own time and background, allowing them to speak with their own authentic voice. This will be true to their own experience of God and so always faithful in opening up the biblical text. But at the same time the series seeks to bring the characters out of the pages of biblical history into our own very different culture. In doing so, the unchanging truths their stories expound and illustrate are applied to the practical business of living for God in the world of the late twentieth century.

Each contributor has been given considerable freedom in their style and treatment of their subject. This is because the range of biblical material is wide and varied, and also it illustrates that opening up and applying the Bible's message does not need to be confined to one style or stereotype. Some writers will be more closely tied to the biblical text than others; but all are united in their common belief in its authority, and therefore its unrivalled relevance. And all are united in their conviction that as we let the Bible speak for our present generation, as for all its predecessors, we shall hear the Word of the Lord, which lasts for ever. This is the prayer with which these books are sent out. I hope you will be able to echo it, and to experience its answer.

D. J. Jackman
Above Bar Church
Southampton

# Introduction

Abraham has always been one of my favourite Old Testament characters. There is something immensely challenging, almost daunting, about a man who could have faith in God when he had no Bible, no background and virtually no fellowship with like-minded individuals. If ever anyone committed himself to believing the bare word of a promising God, it was Abraham. It is little wonder then that he is held up in the New Testament on three occasions as the supreme example of pre-Christian faith: 'Abraham believed God, and it was credited to him as righteousness' (Romans 4:3; Galatians 3:6; James 2:23). Little wonder also that of all the portraits hanging in the gallery of faith-heroes recorded in Hebrews 11, Abraham's is by far the largest and most detailed (Hebrews 11: 8–12, 17–19). But at the same time there is something eminently approachable and ordinary about Abraham, so that he is not only on a pinnacle of excellence far beyond me, but also at my side, a fellow learner in God's school. For Abraham made his mistakes. There are occasions when he failed to believe God, either through stubbornness or ignorance, or just plain rebellion. His record is as etched as ours are with failure and inconsistency, weakness and sin; but above all it bears the marks of God's grace which is determined to make Abraham the man he has chosen him to be – the man who believed God.

A good deal of the groundwork for this biographical study was first done several years ago, in preparation for a series of Sunday evening sermons preached in Above Bar Church, Southampton. I am grateful, as always, to my own church congregation for the stimulus that their appetite for, and attention to, the Word of God provides in my own life week by week. As a church we are committed to the systematic opening up of the Scriptures Sunday by Sunday from the pulpit, and to its outworking in all our smaller group fellowships, as well as in our families and individual lives. I am sure there is no greater need today than for the Spirit of God to take the Word of God in order to equip and strengthen the people of God. In a day when preaching is disregarded by many, I believe that we need above all to rediscover the authentic experience of New Testament Christianity by sitting under the Word of God and submitting our minds and wills to God's revealed truth. Effective preaching is always a dialogue, addressing the hearer from the unchanging foundation of God's Word, but relating and applying that non-negotiable content to all the changing scenes of life, in a society where values are in almost constant flux.

These convictions lie behind the approach of the book. My concern has been to try to understand and explain the story of Abraham's life history so that the reader can work consecutively through the biblical text (Genesis 12–25). I have used the New

International Version of the Bible. But at the same time, and of equal importance, I have also tried to draw out the practical applications for our own walk with God, our own need of faith, in the hope that our contemporary discipleship will be firmly grounded in the Bible's teaching. I hope that my readers may be encouraged to pursue their own Bible study along similar lines.

I should like to thank many who have helped me in this project, not least the officers and members of Above Bar Church, whose generous provision of six months' sabbatical leave in 1986 enabled me to revise and complete this manuscript, among other tasks. To those who have read the manuscript and made a number of very helpful suggestions, to Linda Burt whose patience in interpreting my hieroglyphics in order to type and retype has been amazing, and to Colin Duriez at IVP for his encouragement to me to keep right on to the end, I owe a great debt which I gratefully acknowledge. The shortcomings and inadequacies are entirely my own. Finally I must thank my wife, Heather, and long-suffering family who have not only tolerated my writing project, but actually encouraged and supported me so constantly.

May it be true of us all that the blessing given to Abraham will come to us through Christ Jesus, so that by faith we may receive the promised Holy Spirit (Galatians 3:14).

# Chapter one

# Command and promise

*The Lord had said to Abram, 'Leave your country,
your people and your father's household and go to
the land I will show you.*

> *I will make you into a great
>     nation
>     and I will bless you;
> I will make your name great,
>     and you will be a blessing.
> I will bless those who bless
>     you,
>     and whoever curses you I
>     will curse;
> and all peoples on earth
>     will be blessed through you'*
>           (Genesis 12:1–3).

When we first set out on the Christian life, most of
us have no idea what God is going to do in us or
through us. Peter the fisherman would never have
imagined that one day he would preach to thousands in Jerusalem, become the leader of a great
church in that city and ultimately die as a martyr on

a cross, when first Jesus called him at the lakeside, 'Follow me.' Martin Luther the monk would never have believed you if you had told him that his discovery in the Bible of salvation by God's grace alone, through faith, would sweep through Germany and Scandinavia and change forever the course of European history. Yet more books have been written about Martin Luther in the four centuries since he died than about any other figure in history except Jesus of Nazareth. D. L. Moody, the great evangelist of the last century, had no idea what the outcome would be when he responded to a preacher's challenge that the world had yet to see what God can do with a man who is totally dedicated to him, with the resolve, 'By God's grace, I will be that man.' No doubt you can look back on your own Christian experience and see remarkable changes that have taken place in your life, doors of opportunity that have opened, surprises that God has had in store which you could not have foreseen or even dreamed about when first you began to follow Christ. We can never predict how God will work through an individual, or through a family, either now or in the future.

No-one could have imagined the destiny that lay ahead of Abram. His name first appears in Genesis 11:26 as one among many in a list of generations – just another name, with no special fanfare. But that name represents a person on whose life God had his hand. Although Abram was special in that he was to be the father of God's chosen people, Israel, he is also representative of all those who are prepared to imitate him by trusting the living God. Not surprisingly, the New Testament sees Abram as the great example of faith (see Romans 4: 1–12; Hebrews 11:8–12, 17–19). Great things

14

awaited Abram. But now he is just taking his first faltering steps in the journey of faith. It is a journey that will take him all his life. It's a pilgrimage that will demand everything he has. How can *we* start on that same adventure?

It all begins with *God's call*, and that has two very important ingredients. First of all there is a *command*: 'Leave your country . . . and go to the land I will show you' (verse 1). And then there is a comprehensive *promise*: 'I will make you . . . a great nation . . . I will bless you; I will make your name great, and you will be a blessing' (verse 2).

## The command

Ur was a town with a complex system of government and a well-developed system of commerce, one with writing in common use for the issue of receipts, the making of contracts and many other purposes. There were town drains, streets, two-storied houses, and a great temple tower (Ziggurat), trade routes joining the town with other great towns to the north and south, and various other evidences of a highly developed civilization.*

The command is to leave, to go. It involves a break with the past and a launching out into the future, and the key element is faith. Abram was to leave all the security he enjoyed in Ur of the Chaldeans and to follow God wherever he might lead him, to 'the land I will show you'. It seems that this call had in fact come to Abram some time earlier, but

* J. A. Thompson, *The Bible and Archaeology*, Paternoster, 1973.

15

that his obedience at that stage had been less than complete. The reason why the NIV translates the Hebrew past tense as a pluperfect – 'the Lord *had* said' – is provided in Acts 7:1–3. Here Stephen, on trial for his life before the Sanhedrin, full of the Holy Spirit (Acts 7:55), declares, 'The God of Glory appeared to our father Abraham while he was still in Mesopotamia, before he lived in Haran. "Leave your country and your people," God said, "and go to the land I will show you."' God had told him to leave home and family, but in fact he took his father and his nephew with him. 'Terah', we are told in Genesis 11:31, 'took his son Abram, his grandson Lot son of Haran, and his daughter-in-law Sarai . . . and together they set out from Ur of the Chaldeans to go to Canaan. But when they came to Haran, they settled there.' Since Terah was the senior member of the family he would naturally have had the dominant role ('Terah took his son Abram'). But Genesis 12:1 makes it clear that 'the LORD had said to *Abram*, "Leave your country".' Indeed, the destination had been given, in general terms. They knew they were heading for Canaan, but they settled at Haran. The name means 'crossroads' and the site, near Edessa in Turkey, lay at a strategic point on the main route between Mesopotamia and the west. The culture was similar to that in Ur – both cities were centres of moon worship – and doubtless it was comfortable in Haran. Perhaps Terah, who 'worshipped other gods' (Joshua 24:2), only moved because Ur was under threat from the Elamites, who eventually destroyed it. But for Abram, destiny was beginning to stir, although it was not until Terah died (11:32) that the call was renewed and he was able to move on.

God's call is rarely understood and obeyed fully when we first hear it. Usually it comes over a period of time with increasing persistence and growing clarity. There are often barriers which have to be removed and that cannot be done overnight. While God doesn't want us to neglect our families, his call always implies that he is to have first place in our lives. We have always to balance the Bible's life-long requirement to honour our father and mother (Exodus 20:12) with Jesus' teaching that 'If anyone comes to me and does not hate his father and mother, his wife and children, his brothers and sisters – yes, even his own life – he cannot be my disciple' (Luke 14:26). He has to come first. Whatever our responsibilities to our parents, our responsibility to God is primary. Unless God comes first in our thinking and planning we cannot be people of faith, because the essence of our trust in God is that we should live lives obedient to his will in every detail. So there can be no settling in Haran if God has called us to the land of Canaan. We must move on in obedience to what God says, even if this means separation or misunderstanding from our family. That is why we have to be sure that we really are following God's call, not our own whims and fancies, and why time is always needed to test and confirm it.

## The promise

True faith must have an object – it must be faith in someone or something. And that object must be reliable, worthy of our confidence. You can have great faith and yet be greatly deluded! You can drive your car with great faith in your brake pedal, but if your brakes are faulty you will soon discover

17

how ill-founded your faith was! People can have faith in all sorts of things – religion, money, the stars, politics, education – and they build their lives on sand because ultimately all these things are human and so fallible and quickly changing. Sometimes people say, 'I wish I could have faith like Abram', as though faith was a sort of quantum that some people have and others do not. But faith is not a mystery ingredient of life given to only a few. Faith is acting on evidence before the outcome is seen or proved. We all exercise faith every day we live, when we sit on a chair, or catch a bus, or eat a meal. But because faith needs an object, God gives to Abram the inconceivably great promises of verses 2–3, so that his faith has something firm to grip, something which is rock-solid because God himself is committed to it.

God never commands without promising. Whenever he calls us to himself, whenever he gives us some new task to do, whenever he uproots us and sends us into a new adventure with him, he always helps us to move forward by reminding us of his promises. Through the Bible, through the encouragement of other Christians, by the inner witness of the Holy Spirit, God reveals enough of his own power and faithfulness and sufficient of his purposes for us to take just the next step forward, in faith, and no more. Abram did not receive a map through the letter-box one morning. There were no detailed programmes, no title deeds to his inheritance in Canaan. But there was the unbreakable word of God's promise to stretch and develop his faith and to lead him on. It was the same with Gladys Aylward, the missionary to China, whose remarkable story was told in the film *The Inn of the Sixth Happiness*. Lacking formal education, a parlour maid in London, she knew that God was calling her to China. She was turned down by the missionary societies but she scrimped and saved most of her meagre wages for a number of years until, at about the age of 30, she had enough money to buy a single ticket to China. Her journey took her through Siberia and Japan and eventually to a remote part of China where she opened an inn and told Bible stories. There is much more to her extraordinary life, recorded by Alan Burgess in the book *The Small Woman*; but the point for us is that, like Abram, this twentieth-century woman of faith went one step at a time, doggedly believing and therefore proving God's promises to be utterly reliable.

The promise God gave Abram has two distinct parts to it. First, God announces that Abram will *receive blessing*: 'I will make you into a great nation and I will bless you'. He will become the ancestor of a numerous people and will enjoy both spiritual and material prosperity. Also, he will become a man of influence and honour ('I will make your name great'). The second part of the promise goes much further. Not only will Abram receive blessings, but he will *be a blessing* ('all peoples on earth will be blessed through you'). Indeed, the attitude which the peoples show to Abram will be the attitude God shows to them. Abram is going to be God's representative man.

As we unpack it, we can see that this is a vast promise, by which one solitary individual, Abram, is made into a blessing for multitudes, and all because he responds to God's call to trust and obey him. The peoples of the world who have been cursed, scattered and divided because of sin – all are to be brought within the sphere of God's blessing through the obedience of faithful Abram. We share in that, as his spiritual heirs. For in effect God is saying to him, 'I'm taking a new initiative. I am moving out in grace to heal the divisions between men. I want to create a new humanity, to produce a united family under my fatherhood. I want to change the curse into a blessing for the whole human race.' This is the start of the unfolding of the great promise of grace which we can trace right through the Scriptures to its culmination in the death and resurrection of the Lord Jesus Christ.

## The blessing for us

In his letter to the Galatians Paul reminds us that every Christian stands in the line of the great tradition that runs from Abram, those who are the children of God through faith. These are thrilling assertions.

> The Scripture foresaw that God would justify the Gentiles by faith, and announced the gospel in advance to Abraham: 'All nations will be blessed through you.' So those who have faith are blessed along with Abraham, the man of faith (Galatians 3:8–9).

Or again,

> He redeemed us in order that the blessing given to Abraham might come to the Gentiles through Christ Jesus, so that by faith we might receive the promise of the Spirit (Galatians 3:14).

The chapter concludes,

> If you belong to Christ, then you are Abraham's seed, and heirs according to the promise (Galatians 3:29).

We must never make the mistake of thinking that the Old Testament conflicts with the New, or that its narratives and promises are not for Christians. The whole Bible is one continuous revelation, the whole Word of God for the whole people of God. We Christians, who share Abram's faith, are Abram's descendants. Just as God promised to Abram that he would both receive blessing and be a blessing to countless generations in all the families of the earth, so he promises that through faith in Christ we ourselves, the offspring of Abram, can enter into this very blessing, promised centuries ago. Everyone who turns to God in Christ discovers his grace beginning to transform their lives. This does not mean that life will be free of difficulties. There will sometimes be suffering and sorrow, struggles and problems. These are often the very means by which God blesses us, not just for our own benefit, but in order that we, like Abram, may be a blessing to others. What greater good could we do in anyone's life than to be the channel by which they begin to experience the reality of Christ, who was full of grace and truth (John 1:14)?

When God spoke to Abram all this was way into the future, yet, in a sense, it all hung on this one man's obedience. Our circumstances are totally different, but the principles on which God deals with us still reflect his unchanging character, since equally we are called to trust what he says and, as a result, to live differently. His commands are not always accompanied by reasons, but there are always promises. If God gave us reasons we might not understand them, since his thoughts are higher than our thoughts (Isaiah 55:8–9), but the promises of God are practical, understandable and believable. In fact, every command of God has a promise at its heart, because it reflects his character of love and is designed only for our greatest fulfilment.

## Trust and obey

All this is true from the very beginning of our Christian experience. Perhaps you have been struggling against some of the clear commands of the Bible because of the changes they demand in your priorities or life-style. Perhaps you are fighting God's will for your future, or not really sure you can trust it. Have you realized that when God calls, he always promises? That was how you first became a Christian. There was a command, 'Believe in the Lord Jesus', with a promise, 'and you will be saved' (Acts 16:31). If you obey the command, you will receive the promise. If you believe the promise, you will obey the command. Peter's great sermon at Pentecost has the same pattern. First the command, 'Repent and be baptized . . . in the name of Jesus Christ'. Then the promise, 'And you will receive the gift of the Holy Spirit' (Acts 2:38).

It is not only at the start of the Christian life that this pattern is seen; the thread runs the whole way through. For example, when a Christian is in a real fix, facing great difficulties, how is he to react? There is a command, 'Do not be anxious about anything, but in everything, by prayer and petition, with thanksgiving, present your requests to God.' It is a very clear instruction, and the next verse is full of promise. 'And the peace of God, which transcends all understanding, will guard your hearts and your minds in Christ Jesus' (Philippians 4: 6–7).

The Bible is full of promises – of forgiveness, of new life, of fellowship with God. The first faltering steps of faith are a response to God's command to turn from living for myself, to leave my Ur of the Chaldees, to want God enough to get up and go, by committing my very life to him in the depths of my being. It is as we do this that we begin to receive what God has promised, and that is the secret of the journey right to the end.

Another trap we can easily fall into is that of pretending that Abram was in another league to us. 'I'd love to have a faith like that,' we say, 'but it is not that easy for me.' Because the Bible presents us with the outcome of the struggles of its heroes, we can easily skim-read it and forget, or fail to recognize, the problems and the heartache. There is a stark sentence in Genesis 11:30: 'Now Sarai [Abram's wife] was barren; she had no children.' God has promised to make Abram into a great nation. How does the promise square with the facts? To Abram it must have seemed an insuperable roadblock. He had to live with it for years. He had God's promise of descendants and he had a barren wife. Was it easy for Abram to trust God? He was told to leave all his security behind – for what? For 'the land I will show you'. That was all he knew. But Abram 'believed God'.

Faith acts in obedience and then proves the promise. It rests everything on the reliability of God's word and character. You are not alone if you are feeling that this is too difficult; but if you put God's word to the test and act on what he is saying to you, you will experience his faithfulness. We are like the man who told his young son who

23

was going away to camp for the first time, 'Now don't go into the water until you've learned to swim.' It is an impossibility! You cannot learn to swim unless you entrust yourself to God. You can stand on the brink all your life longing to have a faith like someone else's. Launch out and prove that the promises of God are true! Abram proved them. No-one has ever claimed them and found them false.

Have you ever seen the process by which a spider constructs its web? We marvel at the intricate network of gossamer threads glistening in the sunlight, but how does it all begin? Literally, by jumping off into nowhere. The spider launches itself into the wind, trailing the first thread, and is carried to the anchor point. Everything depends on the first line, which then becomes the route along which the spider travels to weave the whole structure. Without the initial step of faith there would be nothing. So it was with Abram and so it is with us.

God calls us to obey the commands while trusting his promises and he calls us to go on doing it, day by day, throughout our Christian lives. Listen to the call of God!

# Chapter two

# Obedience tested

*So Abram left, as the* LORD *had told him; and Lot went with him. Abram was seventy-five years old when he set out from Haran. He took his wife Sarai, his nephew Lot, all the possessions they had accumulated and the people they had acquired in Haran, and they set out for the land of Canaan, and they arrived there.*

*Abram travelled through the land as far as the site of the great tree of Moreh at Shechem. The Canaanites were then in the land, but the* LORD *appeared to Abram and said, 'To your offspring I will give this land.' So he built an altar there to the* LORD, *who had appeared to him.*

*From there he went on toward the hills east of Bethel and pitched his tent, with Bethel on the west and Ai on the east. There he built an altar to the* LORD *and called on the name of the* LORD. *Then Abram set out and continued towards the Negev.*

*Now there was a famine in the land, and Abram went down to Egypt to live there for a while because the famine was severe. As he was about to enter Egypt, he said to his wife Sarai, 'I know what a beautiful woman you are. When the Eygptians see you, they will say, "This is his wife." Then they will* kill me but will let you live. Say you are my sister, so that I will be treated well for your sake and my life will be spared because of you.'

When Abram came to Egypt, the Eygptians saw that she was a very beautiful woman. And when Pharaoh's officials saw her, they praised her to Pharaoh, and she was taken into his palace. He treated Abram well for her sake, and Abram acquired sheep and cattle, male and female donkeys, menservants and maidservants, and camels.

But the LORD inflicted serious diseases on Pharaoh and his household because of Abram's wife Sarai. So Pharaoh summoned Abram. 'What have you done to me?' he said. 'Why didn't you tell me she was your wife? Why did you say, "She is my sister," so that I took her to be my wife? Now then, here is your wife. Take her and go!' Then Pharaoh gave orders about Abram to his men, and they sent him on his way, with his wife and everything he had (Genesis 12:4–20).


A total change of lifestyle faces Abram. From a settled existence in an established town like Ur or Haran, he is about to embark on the life of a pastoral nomad, travelling up and down through Canaan and its borders, his movements largely affected by the recurring needs of pasture and water for his flocks. We should not think of Abram and his growing clan as desert Bedouin. For the most part they kept to the trade routes, which themselves followed water supplies. But except for Lot they did not settle in towns. They did not farm, at least until Isaac's day (26:12), and then probably rather sporadically. They owned only the land they bought for burial plots. Of course they were neither unique nor original in this way of life. There were many such groups of semi-nomadic herdsmen or stock breeders in those days, moving on foot, their donkeys or camels carrying their food and their children, as they moved from one water supply to another. Travel was virtually unrestricted throughout the fertile crescent and there was constant and easy communication between Egypt and Palestine, through to Syria. The mountainous country within the land of promise, from Shechem south to the Negev, contained many good grazing areas and was still comparatively unpopulated.

This is the way of life Abram is about to adopt as he sets out from Haran at seventy-five years of age (middle life for him, as the story will make clear). We must not underestimate the upheaval and the challenge involved in all this. Hebrews 11:9–10 expresses graphically not only what this life was like, but more importantly the spiritual motivation that got, and kept, him going. 'By faith he made his home in the promised land like a stranger in a foreign country; he lived in tents, as did Isaac and Jacob, who were heirs with him of the same promise. For he was looking forward to the city with foundations, whose architect and builder is God.' He is leaving in obedience to God.

It is significant that the title LORD (Yahweh) is applied to God at the point of his call to Abram (12:1, 4). As the first five books of the Bible (the Pentateuch) develop, more and more meaning is given to this specially revealed personal name of God, reserved for the family of his own chosen people. It carries within it the central idea of God's covenant, or agreement, to be their God and to bless them. So it speaks both of the gracious promises that he freely makes to Abram and his descendants, and also of his faithfulness and power to be able to fulfil them in every situation. It explains why the true response of covenant people must always be to trust and obey the LORD. Disobedience is self-destructive because it blocks all the blessings which God wants to be able to pour into the lives of his people. So, as Abram sets out in obedience on the slow journey from Haran with his property, his animals and the servants he has acquired, he is already the covenant man, acting in obedience to his sovereign ruler, the LORD.

The route into Canaan was marked by sizeable settlements at approximately twenty-mile intervals, with villages in between. As they travelled they were never more than about a day's march from other people or from a water supply. But they had to learn to live a day at a time and to trust God's provision because they did not know how long they would be journeying, or where they would eventually find themselves.

## Walking by faith

What a marvellous picture this gives us of the Christian life! Our journey of faith also means living one day at a time, trusting the Lord, not knowing the future. We don't necessarily understand where God is taking us, or why, nor do we know the details of the journey, but we do know he is reliable and trustworthy, so we obey and follow. We press on each day with what he gives us to do, discovering that he equips and enables us, in the mundane routine as much as in the exciting surprises.

The Bible does not tell us what Abram encountered on the journey. Verse 5 simply mentions that 'they set out for the land of Canaan, and they arrived there'. Scripture is only interested in the strategic things. Undoubtedly the journey took a long time and in all probability a lot happened during it. But we are not told about the crippled donkeys or the limited water supply, just that they arrived. Of course they did, because God called them. He is not in the business of frustrating those whom he invites to venture out with him. But the other factor noted here is their own perseverance. There were plenty of other 'Harans' on the way where they could have settled down, but they kept going God's way until they reached their destination.

'Stickability' is one of the most important qualities we need to develop if ever our lives are going to be really useful to God. There are always plenty of counter-attractions to tempt us, or alternative options to distract us, from doing God's will. Often God permits them precisely to test our faith by seeing whether we will persist in going forward with him, or whether we will give up when the going gets tough and difficult. Only a faith that comes through such tests can be said to be strong and tempered. It's easy to say to God in a warm, cosy meeting, with many other Christians around us, that we will serve him and do whatever he calls us to do. But the proof of that profession can only be seen in perseverance. Think of the Olympic athlete's dedication to the task before him. He has only one aim – to win the gold. But in order to achieve that aim he will put his body through the most rigorous and punishing training schedules, breaking through the pain barriers, building up stamina, day after day, whatever the weather, often while most people are still asleep. His purpose has become the dominant concern of his life, so whatever the temptations to give up he will at all costs keep going. Should our passion to obey God be any less? Abram kept going because he was looking forward to the fulfilment of God's promises and purposes. Every day counts in our Christian lives, and so we need to pray and work for this kind of step-by-step obedience to the Lord. Faithfulness in little things is a very great thing.

So, they reached Shechem (modern-day Nablus), already an important settlement in the central region of Israel. It was situated in the hill country of Ephraim, in the valley that runs between Mount Ebal and Mount Gerizim, about 50 km north of Jerusalem. Here, as they paused in their journey, the LORD appeared to his obedient servant. Perhaps Abram was realizing increasingly that 'the Canaanites were in the land'. They were well settled in. 'This land isn't empty, Lord,' Abram might have prayed. 'This isn't going to be easy. How am I going to possess any of it? What chance does an alien stand here?' The mention of the great tree of Moreh ('Teacher') probably means that it was a site of Canaanite worship. Perhaps this is why the Lord appeared to Abram here. At this point, where doubt might have overwhelmed him, God in his grace renewed the promise and strengthened Abram's faith. 'The LORD appeared to Abram and said, "To your offspring I will give this land." ' Then, for the first time, in response to that renewed promise, an altar to the LORD is built on the land which God is going to give his servant.

Bethel was another 40 or more km south over the hills, and was probably just establishing itself as a prosperous town. Like Shechem, it lies in the zone where the annual rainfall is between 25 and 50 cm. This would indicate that adequate grazing for sheep was available. Here again, out in the hills east of Bethel Abram built an altar to the LORD, reminding himself of all that he was coming to know and prove about the character of Yahweh and dedicating it to him. Abram is acting in faith. He is saying, 'Lord, this land is yours. You have promised to give it to me and I know that you will, because every part of it belongs already to you.' As he moves on in faith, symbolically covering the whole territory, he calls upon God to vindicate his trust and reaffirms his confidence in the promises.

So, he pressed on southwards, towards the Negev. Although the modern usage of this term designates the semi-arid area south-west of the Dead Sea, nearly half the total land area of modern Israel, the biblical usage is not so extensive. Some scholars think the term referred to a fairly narrow east-west strip extending perhaps less than 30 km north and south of Beersheba. Others suggest it designated an area extending as far south as Kadesh-barnea. Either way, it was not the vast area which bears the name 'the Negev' today; but the important fact is that the land was claimed in its entirety for the Lord.

## Abram was only human

If that were the end of the story we could close our Bibles, full of admiration for Abram's triumphant faith. But it might all seem rather remote from our own experience, punctuated as that so often is by failure. However, Abram's story is not an unbroken record of success. Genuine faith is not a matter of moving forward with no problems, mistakes or difficulties. The Bible is far more true to life than that; far more true to human nature –

Abram's, yours and mine. Like us, Abram's faith had to grow through testing. Suddenly, something happened over which Abram had no control and which would challenge both his trust and his obedience. There was a famine in Canaan. Imagine Abram with his family, his slaves, his growing flocks, a stranger in a land of unknown, potentially hostile people where he has absolutely no rights. In a time of famine he is likely to be entirely dependent on the generosity of others, yet many lives depend on him and there is a dwindling food supply. What went through his mind? Had he, after all, made a great mistake? Had God really called him?

Every man or woman of faith is tested in this way. Every new move forward in faith that we make in our Christian lives will be challenged and tested in some way or other. When I first realized that God was calling me out of school-teaching to work for him among students in the universities of Britain, it was an exciting prospect. I remember the exhilaration, mixed with apprehension at the thought of the privilege of being able to devote my time and energy to such a strategic area of Christian service. When the headmaster of the school where I was teaching told me I was a fool and not to come looking for my job back in six months' time, I was able to smile, if a little ruefully. But within those six months, my step of faith was tested and challenged in ways I could hardly have imagined. There was a time when I could easily have thrown in the towel and decided this was not for me, had I not been certain that God had called me. I was so thankful I had no doubts as to what to do at that time. I found myself increasingly praying, 'Lord, I don't know why you've put me here, but I know you have. I think you've got the wrong man, so it's over to you. Your will be done!' I now know that God was developing my faith by stretching it. By showing me in area after area that I was not able, but he was, he was humbling my pride and self-sufficiency and bringing me to the point of dependence where I could begin to be useful. I did not need to ask for my teaching job back!

Was that why the LORD had appeared at Shechem, repeating those two great promises? 'You have no son, but I will give you one. You have no rights, but I will make this land yours.' The Lord had known that the famine was coming and how Abram's faith would be tested by it. So often God renews and confirms his promises to us just because he knows of some testing situation in the future which we have not seen yet, and in his love he is preparing us so that we can hold firm. Such tests come to us all, not because God is angry with us but because he wants to root us more deeply in himself, and he knows that the only way human faith grows is by exercise. When the famine comes, when we face unforeseen pressures, the faithful Christian should not complain or be taken by surprise. That is the very time to be a faith-full Christian and whatever happens, to trust in God. 'Do not be surprised at the painful trial you are suffering, as though something strange were happening to you,' Peter wrote to Christians who were facing Nero's persecutions. 'But rejoice that you participate in the sufferings of Christ, so that you may be overjoyed when his glory is revealed' (1 Peter 4:12–13). And he concludes that 'those who suffer according to God's will should commit themselves to their faithful Creator and continue to do good' (verse 19).

33

So much depends on the perspective from which we look at events. Abram may well have interpreted his first experiences of the promised land quite unfavourably and negatively. It was occupied. He had been shown no place in which to settle. Now there was no food for himself and his dependents, and he still had no heir.

## Going down to Egypt

He reacted to the situation by deciding to overcome the problem himself. He would go on down to Egypt. There was corn in Egypt, so he made for it, although there is no indication that God had told him to leave the land he had promised to him. Humanly speaking, it was a sensible move, and which of us in his situation would have acted differently? 'Let's move while we can, while we have strength, and go where things are better.' But people of faith have to learn that we must stay where God has put us until he gives us a clear call to get up and go. The latter is often the easier. It has all the attraction of the unknown, the surprising, the uncharted. It can be much harder to stay put, immersed in 'the daily round, the common task', especially in a time of famine. But if we move ourselves out of a difficult situation in which God has placed us, we move out of the frying pan into the fire. We shall simply take our problems with us. The pop star who flies off to some exotic destination to 'get away from it all' comes back a fortnight later and reveals, 'I couldn't get away from myself.'

There are Christians who imagine that difficulties in their present job must automatically mean they are being called to change it. I have met young people who have interpreted boredom at work as a call to the mission field, and some who have even been accepted. There are Christian girls who have decided to marry non-Christian men in order to give themselves some imagined security, with disastrous results. There are Christians in business who have entered into shady deals or questionable practices, because they thought they could stave off economic difficulties that way. But that is going down to Egypt for our help. Rather, we must remember that we have a faithful Lord to put between ourselves and our difficulties.

Jesus promised his disciples that when we are concerned above everything else with God's kingdom and what he requires of us, he *will* provide us with food and clothes and everything we really need (Matthew 6:25–34). So often in our panic we forget his promise – or fail to believe it.

However, Abram has begun to slide down a very slippery slope. As his faith fails, his courage disappears. 'As he was about to enter Egypt, he said to his wife . . . "I know what a beautiful woman you are . . . they will say, 'This is his wife' [and] they will kill me [and] let you live. [So] say you are my sister, so that I will be treated well for your sake and my life will be spared"' (12:11–13). What sort of faith is that? Is God going to allow the father of a great nation to be killed in Egypt before the promised son is born? But we don't think in those terms of faith when we begin to move ourselves out of God's will, do we? Reason becomes king; not that faith is ever irrational, but it is often suprarational. The problems loom large. We start trying to cope with them on our own and disaster follows.

There was an element of truth in Abram's statement, for Sarai was his half-sister. He could rationalize it all, but it was his intention to deceive. It was the intention behind his statement that matters, for that is what differentiates a lie from a mistake. When we obscure the truth, or fail to tell the whole truth, deliberately intending to deceive others, we are guilty of lying and that is sin. His worst fears were realized. The King's officials saw Sarai and so praised her to their master that she was taken into his palace. Not only were Abram's fears realized, but now his conscience was weighed down by the shameful awareness that he was buying his own safety at the expense of his wife.

In purely materialistic terms, it worked out splendidly. The King 'treated Abram well for her sake . . . [he] acquired sheep and cattle, male and female donkeys, menservants . . . maidservants . . . camels' (verse 16). He was apparently prospering in his disobedience, but it was only a temporal, material prosperity. His wealth belonged to this world alone. It was subject to change and to decay and he would have to leave it all behind in the end. Of course it's very possible to throw Christian principles (caricatured as 'scruples') overboard and to do very well materially. But real prosperity is spiritual and eternal. 'How much did your father leave?' the reporters asked the multi-millionaire's son after the will was read. 'All of it,' was the absolutely truthful reply. Abram came to understand that he could build no altar to Yahweh in Egypt. There was no walk with God there, no revelations of the divine character, no renewal of the divine promises. He prospered materially but at the expense of his spiritual wealth.

## God doesn't give up

Yet even in this situation of compromise God is faithful to his promises, in spite of Abram's failure to trust. Nothing will be allowed to hinder their eventual fulfilment, not even the faithlessness of the man who is being trained to believe God. Abram may drift down into Egypt and make mistake upon mistake, but God has not, and will not, let Abram go. And so 'the LORD inflicted serious diseases on Pharaoh and his household because of Abram's wife' (verse 17). Inevitably it all comes out. The shame of Abram's sin is revealed and he is drummed out of Eygpt in a hurry and not a little disgrace. We can almost hear the King yelling, 'Here's your wife – take her and get out!' (verse 19). The man of faith is shown up by a pagan monarch.

If all else fails, God may use suffering to bring us to our senses, and sometimes that suffering is seen in the lives of other people who have been affected by our sin. A man may convince himself that he does not have a problem with his temper until one day he strikes out and injures someone. A wagging tongue can be justified as harmless until one day someone's suicide attempt alerts us to the terrible suffering which gossip can produce. Perhaps if we realized more readily that none of our sinning is done in a vacuum, we would be a less easy prey to temptation.

But with God, even abject failure like Abram's does not mean the scrap-heap. If it did, where would any of us be? We don't find it hard to identify with Abram's probable feelings – shame, failure, fear, doubt. Could God ever forgive him? Could he be restored? Would God still fulfil his purpose for him? We have all been there ourselves, and the more spiritually sensitive we are, the more often we feel it. Nevertheless, God is committed to his servant and he will get him back on track. It may be costly, even hurtful, and the route may be unpleasant, but God will not leave us off course, either. The tragedy of sin is that it leads us into all sorts of problems and difficulties which we may have to live with for a long time. While he freely and fully forgives our guilt, we are not always, or automatically, rescued from the consequences of our sin, because we live in a world structured by God where causes lead to effects. Broken relationships cannot be rebuilt overnight. Trust that has been betrayed takes time to be renewed. Wrong attitudes, ingrained over years, are not wiped out at a stroke. Habits of righteousness have to be acquired, just as sinful ones were. But God is on our side. He loves us too much to allow us to continue in our unbelief. And if God can use raw material like Abram to make his 'friend', then we should aspire to that high calling too – whatever our failures, however faltering our faith.

Nothing was going to thwart God's purposes for Abram. His disobedience was going to make the outworking of those plans more difficult for him, as we shall see, but it was not going to end the covenant. Although that relationship was imposed unilaterally upon Abram by God's grace, we must remember that Abram was a man of faith, not a fatalist. He was called, as we are, to co-operate with God's work in his life, not to be a blind pawn in his hands. Abram's plight was not inevitable. If God has called us, and if we have responded and are living in daily contact with him, growing in faith each day, we don't *need* to go down to Egypt. We don't have to drift off track. We can keep pace with God's plans, because as we take one step, he will show us the next. So many of our problems come because we want to see twenty steps further on and are not content to take this step, in faith, unless we do. But faith is going a step at a time without seeing the whole journey or knowing the full story. If we trust him and obey him, God will not only bless us with his salvation and make us a blessing to other people, but he will go on stretching that faith, developing all the potential he has put within us, and making us the people he wants us to be so that we can fulfil the purposes of God in our own generation.

# Chapter three

# Our choices matter

*So Abram went up from Egypt to the Negev, with his wife and everything he had, and Lot went with him. Abram had become very wealthy in livestock and in silver and gold.*

*From the Negev he went from place to place until he came to Bethel, to the place between Bethel and Ai where his tent had been earlier and where he had first built an altar. There Abram called on the name of the LORD.*

*Now Lot, who was moving around with Abram, also had flocks and herds and tents. But the land could not support them while they stayed together, for their possessions were so great that they were not able to stay together. And quarrelling arose between Abram's herdsmen and the herdsmen of Lot. The Canaanites and Perizzites were also living in the land at that time.*

*So Abram said to Lot, 'Let's not have any quarrelling between you and me, or between your herdsmen and mine, for we are brothers. Is not the whole land before you? Let's part company. If you go to the left, I'll go to the right; if you go to the right, I'll go to the left.'*

*Lot looked up and saw that the whole plain of*

*the Jordan was well watered, like the garden of the
LORD, like the land of Egypt, toward Zoar. (This
was before the LORD destroyed Sodom and
Gomorrah.) So Lot chose for himself the whole
plain of the Jordan and set out towards the east. The
two men parted company: Abram lived in the land
of Canaan, while Lot lived among the cities of the
plain and pitched his tents near Sodom. Now the
men of Sodom were wicked and were sinning greatly
against the LORD.*

*The LORD said to Abram after Lot had parted
from him, 'Lift up your eyes from where you are
and look north and south, east and west. All the land
that you see I will give to you and your offspring for
ever. I will make your offspring like the dust of the
earth, so that if anyone could count the dust, then
your offspring could be counted. Go, walk through
the length and breadth of the land, for I am giving
it to you.'*

*So Abram moved his tents and went to live near
the great trees of Mamre at Hebron, where he built
an altar to the LORD* (Genesis 13:1–18).

Like a muscle, faith grows by being used, tested,
tried, and then stretched a little bit further. That
is what is happening in this chapter, where the new
test concerns a choice which faces Abram. This
time, as we shall see, he comes through the test
triumphantly.

After his failure in Egypt, Abram retraces his
steps to the Promised Land. He knows where he is
going. Forging up north, he makes for the place
out in the hills between Bethel and Ai where he
had earlier built an altar. He knows he has to get
back on to God's track. So he returns to the place

where his faith was strong, where he knew the Lord's presence and the Lord's blessing. The altar, for Abram, was a place of rededication.

This is an important lesson in the life of faith. When we have gone wrong, whether through ignorance or through our own wilful rebellion; when we have tried to do God's work in our own way; when we have imagined that we know better than he does; when we have gone down into Egypt – then we have to get back to the point where we broke fellowship with God. We need to get back to the place where we knew him and were in real communion with him, where we were able to call on his name, to trust and worship him. We need to go back to our altar – a wooden cross, where atonement was made once for all. The only way back to usefulness for a Christian who has strayed from God's path is through the cross. That means repentance, because I cannot come to that altar either trusting in myself or continuing my rebellion against God. It means submission as I confess my sin and failure, and receive at the cross the cleansing and pardon I so much need. Only then can my life be open to the power and grace of the risen Lord.

By getting back on course and renewing his own covenant faithfulness in his relationship with Yahweh, Abram was preparing for the next test that was to come to him, preparing the way for victory. Of course that was only possible because of the character of the Lord on whose name he called. All our victories are his. The LORD is the God who, by his own sovereign will, chooses to involve himself with people and then commits himself to the people he chooses. He brings his grace into their lives and gives them mercy when they deserve nothing but wrath. He directs their paths, corrects their wanderings and brings them into an increasingly deep dependence and ever closer relationship with himself. God's children may be knocked down on their pilgrimage, but they are never knocked out, because the Lord himself lifts up the downcast, and strengthens those who cannot help themselves. So God restored Abram.

By now he was a wealthy man, for it seems that Sarai's dowry had not been recalled. The King of Egypt was so keen to see them gone that he let them take everything he had given them. Yet it was from that wealth that Abram's next problem was about to appear. Perhaps we should not use the word 'problem'. What we see as 'problems', God sees as opportunities to prove his grace and mercy – all that is meant by his covenant faithfulness and his power to act in human lives. The Bible is full of stories relating how God converted problems into opportunities for his people by stepping in personally. God specializes in what we call impossibilities. The story of this next 'test' or 'opportunity' involves three choices: Abram's, Lot's, and God's.

## Abram's choice

After Terah's death, when Abram left Haran, his nephew Lot was among the party that accompanied him. He also had flocks and tents and a number of herdsmen who worked for him. As God prospered both men and their resources developed, it became increasingly difficult to find adequate pasture for so many animals and such a large travelling unit. The herdsmen were each committed to their own boss and wanted to do their best for him, so it was

43

not long before friction developed and quarrelling broke out between the two groups. Other tribes were in the vicinity, competing for the same resources and only too glad to benefit from any strife among their rivals. So, Abram wisely suggests to Lot that they part, and then takes a great step of faith by not exercising his right as the senior man to direct Lot as to where he should go. Rather he uses his freedom of choice to allow Lot to choose. He acts on the principle that since Lot and he are close relatives, continuing division and hostility would be destructive to them both. Abram could not do anything to remove the cause of the friction – the shortage of pasture – but he could deal with its results as quickly and generously as possible. So Abram decided to let Lot choose which area he wanted for himself.

Why was that? Lot seems to have been rather a weak character. He had been travelling along in Abram's wake, benefiting from all that his uncle had learned and experienced, but there is no indication that he ever took the initiative himself. Perhaps, therefore, Abram was trying to encourage Lot to grow as a person and to learn to depend on God for himself. He was placing Lot in a position where he would be forced to exercise responsibility and make his own choices. As for himself, Abram knew that if he put Lot's interests first, God would take care of the consequences for him. One thing he had learned from the Egyptian adventure was that God had pledged himself to care for Abram and bring him into his inheritance. He had also learned that the best way forward was not to calculate how he could bring all this about for himself, and not to act on his own inadequate understanding, much less on the basis of fear, but simply to trust God. So Abram came to the conclusion that Lot could not rob him of what his faithful God had promised. Therefore, he could put Lot first, allow him to choose and in that choice let God choose for him.

His faith is growing before our eyes. By faith he left, first Ur and then Haran; by faith he claimed the land of which he owned nothing; by faith he now trusts God for an unseen future. This is a great example to us. A Christian who is sure of God is able to hold lightly to the things of this world. He knows that everything he has comes from God's grace. So his hands are off the controls of his life and he becomes a person whose characteristic response is to give generously rather than to grab selfishly. And that is practical, down-to-earth faith. 'Lord, open the right door for me and close the wrong ones. I will go through the doors you open and I won't try to beat down the doors you close. Lord, my life is in your hands. You choose my inheritance.' Abram gave the choice of his future not only to Lot, but supremely to the sovereign God.

## Lot's choice

'Lot looked up and saw that the whole plain of the Jordan was well watered . . . so Lot chose for himself the whole plain of the Jordan . . . and the two men parted company' (verses 10–11). Picture Abram and Lot surveying the country from their vantage point on the heights of Bethel. On three sides they would see very little to attract a shepherd's eye, for that land was largely barren hill country, with only limited grazing potential. But they knew that to the south-east ran the River

Jordan, meandering over a wide plain. This was lush and fertile ground. As the Jordan would not have been visible from the region of Bethel, it is probable that Abram and Lot travelled the area and did a thorough reconnaissance job before the choice was made. It reminded them of Eden, 'the garden of the Lord'. It recalled to their minds what they had seen of Egypt with its overflowing River Nile and its fertility. This was a good and prosperous land.

Of course it appealed to Lot. He looked up and saw, and had no second thoughts. He chose on the basis of what he thought would be most beneficial for him. How he could prosper materially! How well he would be able to support himself and his family! There is no record of him stopping to ask what God wanted, or of his consulting him about his choice. He acted in self-confidence and probably in selfishness, eager to do the best he could for himself. But he did not keep to the lush pasture by the river. Soon we find Lot settled among the cities in the valley, near Sodom whose people 'were wicked and were sinning greatly against the LORD' (verse 13). By Genesis 19, we find him living within the city and acting as one of its elders, sucked into the vortex of Sodom.

Our choices do matter even though we sometimes try to argue that they don't. But there is a process, a sequence to the chain of cause and effect, thought and action, about which the Bible wants us to be realistic. We choose to entertain a thought and it becomes an action. We choose to perform that action and it becomes a habit. We choose our habits and they shape our character. We choose a character and find it leads us to a destiny.

Our choices do matter. But how many Christians

really do ask God to choose where they will live? It is all too easy to choose on the basis of other things – the desirability of the house, the quality of the neighbourhood, good schools, easy transport, closeness to friends. All of these are perfectly worthy in themselves, but the overriding questions should be, 'Where does God want me to be? What about God's plans and my commitment to doing his will in my life?' This is not to deny that one of the means God uses to guide us is the circumstances of our everyday lives, over which he is, after all, sovereign. But the fact that a door opens is not, in and of itself, proof that it is God's way forward for us. There are other factors to bear in mind, not least of which is our own personal motivation for the course of action we are proposing, measured against the character of God revealed in his commands in Scripture.

Lot's choice was dictated by the prospect of material gain rather than by the will of God. The two are not mutually exclusive, as Abram's life shows us, but the latter must always be our priority. Lot also chose to become progressively caught up in the life of Sodom. He chose friends who did not believe in his God and whose lifestyle was in flagrant rebellion against him. Some Bible commentators have speculated that Lot wanted to tell the people of Sodom about the Lord and so he joined them to be a witness, as God's salt and light in that city. But the Bible does not say that was Lot's motive. He seems to have chosen Sodom, not because he wanted to be a 'friend of sinners' in the sense that Jesus was, in order to turn people from their sin, but because he enjoyed their company and their lifestyle. Certainly Sodom needed a witness to the reality of the living God, but if God

47

had taken Lot to Sodom and called him to be that witness he would have kept Lot close to himself and free from Sodom's wickedness. God can keep us anywhere if he takes us there, but not if we make that choice irrespective of his will. There is a separation from sin which faith recognizes and accepts, as Lot should have done, but a person who is walking by sight (by his senses) rather than by faith will not discern it. The same Jesus who was willing to eat and drink with sinners was also 'holy, blameless, pure, set apart from sinners' (Hebrews 7:26).

Lot's basic mistake was that he was not prepared to trust God. He wanted to make his own way and so he was irresistibly drawn to Sodom, and the rest of his life is a very sad story. His daughters married men of the city. Later he was taken captive, his property was destroyed and his wife was turned to a pillar of salt.

Our jobs, our friendships, what we do with our spare time – all this matters. If we know God as our Father and the Lord Jesus as our Saviour, then it is both our responsibility and our privilege to cry out to him for guidance and direction in our lives, so that we do make our choices within his will. If we selfishly head for the valley and Sodom beyond it, we put ourselves outside of God's will and store up for ourselves bitterness and sadness of heart. Sometimes we try to justify wanting our own way by asking, 'Well, what is wrong with it?' But that is a very negative way to make a decision about anything. Rather, we should be asking, 'Is this positively good and right?', and even more important, 'Is this God's will for me?' Christianity is not a matter of doing what is 'not wrong', it is a matter of devoting your life to God's perfect will. Pray about the choices facing you – which course of study to follow, which career to pursue, where to live and work, whom to marry, which form of Christian service and outreach to get involved in, or whatever other decision you may have to make. Discover God's will and do it.

## God's choice

After the decision has been made, God responds to Abram's faith. This is entirely characteristic of the covenant-keeping God who chooses always to bless and prosper his obedient servants. In some ways the separation between Abram and Lot was actually the final stage in Abram's obedience to God's earlier command (12:1) to sever the family ties. Now God meets this new obedience by giving Abram a view of reality very different from Lot's. When Lot looked around he only had eyes for the well-watered plain. But now God tells Abram to look out over the same panorama. As Abram surveys the whole land in every direction, north and south, east and west, God promises it all to him and his descendants. Lot may occupy the land but God owns it and he gives it to whom he wills. How much better it is to wait until God reveals his plans than to rush ahead, like Lot, in selfishness and unbelief. If we give ourselves over to God's will, he will look after our interests far better than we ever could. This is part of his covenant care; he has pledged himself to do it.

Notice too how the content of the promise is becoming increasingly clear. At first, the precise and detailed geographical location of the land had not been specified: 'Go to the land that I will show you and I will be with you.' Now God is saying to

Abram, in effect, 'This is it! Here is what I promised you.' And the terms of the promise are more focused: 'All the land that you see I will give to you and your offspring for ever' (13:15). Abram hasn't even got a residence visa in the land, much less a son to ensure that he will have descendants, but he demonstrates his faith in God by acting on his word. ' "Go, walk through the length and breadth of the land, for I am giving it to you." So Abram moved his tents' (verse 17). Here was a tangible foretaste of the fulfilment of the promise. God had chosen to give him this land. So, he explores and enjoys the land that is his.

Entering more fully into all that God has chosen to give his servant is seen, then, as the direct fruit of faith. It's a journey that can only be undertaken one step at a time, but each step will take us deeper into the land, and as we begin to penetrate it we discover that its length and breadth are vaster than we have ever imagined. We may feel that Abram had advantages that we don't have. After all, God spoke to him in very concrete terms and in an unmistakable way. But stop and think! We have a whole Bible in which God speaks to us, sixty-six books crammed full of his promises and instructions. We have the Holy Spirit living within us to teach us the truth and to help us believe, to show us just how deeply God loves us in Jesus. We are so much more privileged than even Abram was.

God does not have favourites. His resources are equally available to all his people. He deals with us all on the same terms. If we want to know God's blessing in the details of our lives, then we must trust and obey him in the details of our lives. Some Christians, however, appropriate God's resources more fully and more faithfully than others. They walk through the land God has given them. They explore its farthest dimensions. They experience and enjoy its riches more deeply. Because they appeal to God whenever they are in need, they discover his all-sufficiency again and again. And they are more obedient.

When Abram moved his tents in obedience to the Lord, he settled for the time being near Hebron (meaning 'confederacy' or 'fellowship'), the highest town in Israel, some 30 km south-west of Jerusalem. The local population were Hittites (10:15), the sons of Heth. Abram took up residence just outside and to the north of the town at Mamre, where he was to spend considerable periods of his life. Then he built an altar to the LORD (13:18). We too need to build fresh altars of dedication, to bring to the Lord the living sacrifice of bodies and minds devoted to do his will. We need constantly to be renewing our commitment to God. It was said of Bishop Taylor Smith that every morning, on waking, he would pray, 'Lord, here I am; this bed is your altar and I am your sacrifice. Take me and do with me whatever you will today.' That is the only way to live as a Christian – to give ourselves consistently to God's service, to renew our dedication at the start of every day. God has chosen to commit himself to those who trust him and obey him.

# Chapter four

# Blessing through battles

*At this time Amraphel king of Shinar, Arioch king of Ellasar, Kedorlaomer king of Elam and Tidal king of Goiim went to war against Bera king of Sodom, Birsha king of Gomorrah, Shinab king of Admah, Shemeber king of Zeboiim, and the king of Bela (that is, Zoar). All these latter kings joined forces in the Valley of Siddim (the Salt Sea). For twelve years they had been subject to Kedorlaomer, but in the thirteenth year they rebelled.*

*In the fourteenth year, Kedorlaomer and the kings allied with him went out and defeated the Rephaites in Ashteroth Karnaim, the Zuzites in Ham, the Emites in Shaveh Kiriathaim and the Horites in the hill country of Seir, as far as El Paran near the desert. Then they turned back and went to En Mishpat (that is, Kadesh), and they conquered the whole territory of the Amalekites, as well as the Amorites who were living in Hazezon Tamar.*

*Then the king of Sodom, the king of Gomorrah, the king of Admah, the king of Zeboiim and the king of Bela (that is, Zoar) marched out and drew up their battle lines in the Valley of Siddim against Kedorlaomer king of Elam, Tidal king of Goiim,*

*Amraphel king of Shinar and Arioch king of Ellasar – four kings against five. Now the Valley of Siddim was full of tar pits, and when the kings of Sodom and Gomorrah fled, some of the men fell into them and the rest fled to the hills. The four kings seized all the goods of Sodom and Gomorrah and all their food; then they went away. They also carried off Abram's nephew Lot and his possessions, since he was living in Sodom.*

*One who had escaped came and reported this to Abram the Hebrew. Now Abram was living near the great trees of Mamre the Amorite, a brother of Eshcol and Aner, all of whom were allied with Abram. When Abram heard that his relative had been taken captive, he called out the 318 trained men born in his household and went in pursuit as far as Dan. During the night Abram divided his men to attack them and he routed them, pursuing them as far as Hobah, north of Damascus. He recovered all the goods and brought back his relative Lot and his possessions, together with the women and the other people.*

*After Abram returned from defeating Kedorlaomer and the kings allied with him, the king of Sodom came out to meet him in the Valley of Shaveh (that is, the King's Valley).*

*Then Melchizedek king of Salem brought out bread and wine. He was priest of God Most High, and he blessed Abram, saying,*

*'Blessed be Abram by God
    Most High,
    Creator of heaven and
        earth.
And blessed be God Most
    High,*

who delivered your enemies<br>
into your hand.'

*Then Abram gave him a tenth of everything.*

*The king of Sodom said to Abram, 'Give me the people and keep the goods for yourself.'*

*But Abram said to the king of Sodom, 'I have raised my hand to the LORD, God Most High, Creator of heaven and earth, and have taken an oath that I will accept nothing belonging to you, not even a thread or the thong of a sandal, so that you will never be able to say, "I made Abram rich." I will accept nothing but what my men have eaten and the share that belongs to the men who went with me – to Aner, Eshcol and Mamre. Let them have their share'* (Genesis 14:1–24).

In the last chapter we looked at a very personal domestic situation, in which a man and his nephew decided to face their difficulties and settle their differences by going their separate ways. Neither of them could have anticipated how quickly what had seemed so full of promise for Lot would be lost, nor how Abram's apparently inferior prospects would be used in God's hand not only to bless the man himself, but also to be a means of blessing to Lot and many others.

For the first time in Abram's story we are introduced to certain unfolding events in which he has no part to play, at least in their beginning. But as always in Bible history, the interest centres not simply in the events themselves, but in what God is doing in the man of faith whom he is painstakingly constructing. The Bible's concern is not so much with a detailed historical account as with the spiritual significance of the incidents it records. So while this chapter features a true contemporary event, the major focus continues to be on God's dealing with Abram. Nevertheless, we can have every confidence that we are dealing here with history.

The story is of a battle of the four kings against the five. Alliances of kings like this are a well-established feature of Mesopotamian history in the early part of the second millenium BC. There is evidence of as many as twenty kings being allied together.* The leader of the four seems to have been Kedorlaomer of Elam, the name given to the Plain of Khuzistan, just north of the Persian Gulf. It is known that at this time there was a strong Elamite dynasty which actually destroyed and sacked the city of Ur. This powerful ruler, like many after him attracted by the strategic position of Israel, swept down the Jordan valley from the north, conquering the cities that lay in his way, and so was able to dominate the key trade route between Syria and Egypt. Rich pickings were to be had from the levies which could be imposed on the merchant traffic between Asia and Africa and collected from the vassal city-states. For twelve years the five cities of the plain had paid him tribute, but in the thirteenth they rebelled. So Kedorlaomer had to undertake a further invasion to reassert his authority.

Wisely, he combines forces with three other kings from the Euphrates valley, gathering reinforcements as he goes. Down he swoops through the north of the country, mopping up opposition as he travels. Gradually the tribes living

* K. A. Kitchen, *Ancient Orient and Old Testament*, London, 1966, p. 45.

55

in the hill country across the Jordan fall to his invasion (verses 5–6). Then he turns his attention to the southern Negev, in the area of Kadesh, the Amalekite and Amorite territories, which are also subdued (verse 7). Finally, having effectively surrounded them, the cities of the plain face the might of Kedorlaomer's war machine. In this way he is able to pull the net in gradually, until at last only the five rebellious cities are left to be dealt with. It is a sound military strategy.

At last the battle lines are drawn up in the Valley of Siddim (salt), an area which was later submerged under the Salt (Dead) Sea. Most of the southern end of the Dead Sea seems to have developed since Roman times and previous civilizations are sunk without trace. Even at this time it was clearly very difficult terrain on which to fight, since it was full of bitumen pits, one after another. Whether the five kings waited too long until there was no more favourable battle site, or whether they had confidence on their home ground, we don't know, but clearly they were routed. The greater strength of the invaders (they probably had chariots and certainly horses) put an end to the vassal kings' defiance. Their armies fled, some to the hills and some into the pits. Sodom and Gomorrah seem to have fared worst, the undefended towns being plundered for prisoners as well as food and possessions. And as the conquerors began the long journey north, among the captives was a man named Lot. The mood among the victors must have been elation. Certainly it was a long trek back and they had a great deal to load them down. It had been a demanding campaign, but everything had gone to plan. They were tired after the battle and the preceding skirmishes, but they were in no hurry because they were in no danger. They had plenty to show for their hard work.

But unknown to them as they journeyed home, 'one who had escaped came and reported this to Abram' (verse 13). Perhaps he had originally been one of the herdsmen who had left with Lot and gone with him down to the plain of Jordan and then on to Sodom. It seems very likely, because he certainly knew where to find Abram and where to find help. Abram is about to become involved in an event which will lead him to a personal encounter with three kings.

## Encounter with Kedorlaomer

There seems to have been no hesitation whatever in Abram's reaction to the news of the disaster. At one level this is explicable in terms of the culture of which Abram was a part. The eastern concept of the family unit was much stronger than ours is today in the west, so that Abram would have seen himself as head of the 'household', which still included Lot. His role was to act as protector of all who were members of that unit and in that capacity he would have felt *obliged* to act anyway. But I do not think it is fanciful to see a deeper level operating here as well. Abram knows that God has called him, the one man, to be a blessing to many. On that score too there can be no indifference, no arrogance.

There is also none of the attitude that Lot has made his own bed and must lie on it. Instantly he calls out and arms his men, all 318 of them. This was quite a private army, giving us some idea of how large the Abram 'corporation' had grown by this time and a measure of how greatly God had blessed him. He calls on the covenant of friendship, probably a mutual defence treaty, which he had made with some of the other local clan leaders, Mamre and his brothers Eshcol and Aner, and, for Lot's sake, they set off in hot pursuit of Kedorlaomer's home-going forces.

Catching up with them at Dan in the far north of the country, near the springs of the Jordan, Abram decides to divide his forces, and in the well-planned surprise of a night attack from several quarters he wins a great victory, although he must have been considerably outnumbered. Indeed, it was a rout, with the invaders chased as far as Hobah, way beyond Damascus. They left all their booty behind as they fled, so Abram was able to make a total recovery of people, including Lot, and possessions. Kedorlaomer escaped with his life, but he was a defeated man.

God was with Abram, guiding his choices, directing his plans, and above all accomplishing his will. Abram was living in harmony with that will, so that when the emergency arose, he was the man whom God could use to rescue the citizens of Sodom. The contrast with Lot shouts at us from the story. Lot went to the extreme of total identification with the godless society around him, with the result that he was useless to God. As Christians we shall not rescue our dying world by becoming virtually indistinguishable from it. Nor shall we be of any use to God if we become so remote from the world that we no longer care about it or want to be involved. Abram could have been completely isolated and he would have been equally useless. But Abram's faith prevented him from going to either extreme. The Good Shepherd goes after his lost sheep, as Abram went after Lot, but it was his close contact with God that gave Abram the courage, compassion and commitment to bother. Our outreach as Christians into the world of need all around us will only be effective if it is the overflow of the life of God within us. In our generation too we are called to go out and do battle on the side of righteousness against evil, in many different areas of society. We have not been called to a picnic. There is a war on against the world, the flesh and the devil, but only men and women of faith who are close enough to God, see the opportunities in the conflict and prayerfully win through. If we face very little opposition it could be that we are so conditioned and moulded by the prevailing ethos of our society that there is nothing to attack. It is not difficult for us to become spiritual noncombatants, utterly ordinary, savourless salt. Or, on the other hand, we can grow apathetic and cold, detached, on the outskirts of life, unmoved and unconcerned about the people around us. Between these two extremes lies the way of faith and therefore of effectiveness. With courage, through prayer, and by counting our own comfort as less important than the well-being of those whom we want to rescue, we can be used, as Abram was, in God's victories.

## Encounter with the king of Sodom

'After Abram returned from defeating Kedorlaomer . . . the king of Sodom came out to meet him . . . [and] said, "Give me the people and keep the goods for yourself" ' (verses 17, 21). This may well have been a more difficult battle for Abram. It was certainly more strategic. Having heard of Abram's victory, the king came out of hiding and made what looked like an irresistible offer to Abram. Was it done out of gratitude or generosity? Or was he motivated by fear? Perhaps he was trying to curry favour with Abram, afraid that the conqueror of Kedorlaomer might take advantage of his position and carry on where his victim had left off, as Sodom's overlord. But whatever the motivation it must have been a tempting offer. And what could possibly be wrong with it? It was the king's to give, and if Abram had accepted it he would probably have become the most wealthy and powerful clan chief in the region. Was this part of the 'blessing' that God had promised?

In such circumstances, Abram's response is astonishing. 'I have raised my hand to the LORD, God Most High, Creator of heaven and earth, and have taken an oath that I will accept nothing belonging to you, not even a thread or the thong of a sandal, so that you will never be able to say, "I made Abram rich." '

What a reply! I would love to have seen the expression on the king of Sodom's face. Abram had already anticipated this offer and he had already worked out his attitude and taken up his position. Nothing was going to be allowed to take glory from the Lord his God – nothing. Look at the faith and love that are contained in the names and descriptions of God which he uses. He knows God to be always faithful to his covenant promises, always gracious and always dependable. He is God the all-powerful, over whom there is nothing and no-one. He is God the creator, who made and owns and sustains everything. Only God can make Abram rich. Only he possesses heaven and earth. No-one is going to be able to say it was the king of Sodom who prospered this great man of faith. So he has not the slightest hesitation in turning down what might appear on the surface to be a very attractive proposition.

It is interesting also to contrast Abram's behaviour on this occasion with his willingness to accept all that Pharaoh had thrust upon him following the debacle in Egypt. This had made him 'very wealthy in livestock and in silver and gold' (13:2). Perhaps this was a specially tender point with Abram's conscience and so he determined not to allow that process to be repeated, however legitimate it might appear to be, on this occasion.

It is all too easy to compromise and by so doing to lose all that matters most. Just one deceptive business move, for personal gain, but it can be enough to trap an individual and destroy any influence for God. A favour received can so easily spell a bondage ahead. The answer to the temptation is to see that we do not need the world's favours to enrich us. We have the living God who gives his children all things richly to enjoy and provides us daily with all that we really need. But only someone who believes that can say 'No' to the enticing offers of the king of Sodom. It does not have to be money that tempts us. It can equally be status, prestige or influence within a particular circle. If we are prepared to adapt our 'inflexible' attitude or lower our 'unreasonable' standards, to move a little towards the non-Christian way of looking at things, then we could be really 'on the inside', really accepted and one of them, and all sorts of enrichments might come our way, it is hinted. It all sounds so reasonable that only the eye of faith can see the trap.

Yet Abram's faith was never other-worldly and pious. He was always a realist. 'I will accept nothing but what my men have eaten and the share that belongs to the men who went with me' (verse 24). He will make not a pennyworth of personal profit from this venture, but he will accept proper payment for his own men and for his allies. Faith and naïvety do not belong together. Abram followed a Lord who would teach a later generation of disciples to be 'as shrewd as snakes and as innocent as doves' because he was sending them out 'like sheep among wolves' (Matthew 10:16). We need to tread in the same footprints.

## Encounter with Melchizedek

I have put this encounter last because it is the key to the other two, though actually it occurred before the king of Sodom made his offer. 'Then Melchizedek king of Salem brought out bread and wine. He was priest of God Most High, and he blessed Abram' (14:18–19a). 'Then Abram gave him a tenth of everything' (verse 20b). He is a mysterious figure, this king of Salem (probably Jerusalem), whose own name means 'king of righteousness'. He appears from nowhere to receive homage from Abram and to be the channel of God's renewed blessing to his faithful servant, and within three verses disappears again. We know nothing about his ancestry, his birth, his reign or his death, except that he was priest of God Most High, that is, the true and living God, since the title 'God Most High' is directly related to the LORD, Yahweh, in Abram's statement to the king of Sodom (verse 22). So here, apparently, was one godly man, apart from Abram's line, carrying on the worship of Yahweh in the city of Salem ('peace') as both priest and king.

Interestingly, his name occurs again in two other books of the Bible. In Psalm 110:4 a king in David's line is proclaimed by divine decree 'a priest for ever, in the order of Melchizedek'. David had conquered Jerusalem and had therefore become heir to Melchizedek's throne. But as the centuries passed and the monarchy faded, hope of the fulfilment of the promise centred on a coming king, a future Messiah sent from God, who would exercise the twin ministries of priest and king. So in the New Testament letter to the Hebrews the writer expounds the fulfilment of the promise in the person and work of the Lord Jesus. Part of the purpose of that fascinating letter is to prove the superiority of Christ to all the Old Testament provisions and therefore of his priesthood to the old levitical order of priests. To do this, we are taken back by the writer to the picture we have here in Genesis. Normally, the priests collected tithes from the people – they did not pay them. But those very priests were descended from Levi, who was descended from Abram. So the writer imagines the whole levitical priesthood as yet unborn, still in the body of their ancestor Abram as he bows to Melchizedek, gives a tenth and receives a blessing. In this way, the old priesthood in Abram acknowledged the superiority of the eternal priesthood of Melchizedek, which has now been perfectly fulfilled in Jesus Christ, our great and eternal high priest (see Hebrews 7:1–19). In Melchizedek we are surely meant to see one of the earliest foreshadowings of Christ.

For one thing, Melchizedek combined the office of priest and king in his own person. That was unique in the Old Testament. The levitical priesthood was strictly separated from the monarchy,

and when King Uzziah tried to usurp the function
of the priesthood by offering incense at the temple
altar, he was struck down with leprosy (see 2
Chronicles 26:16–21). But those two rigidly separated offices were perfectly combined in Christ. The
priests could only offer animal sacrifice, over and
over again, in the temple, for their own sins and
those of the people; Christ 'did not enter by means
of the blood of goats and calves; but he entered
the Most Holy Place once for all by his own blood'
(Hebrews 9:12). Again, 'Christ did not enter a
man-made sanctuary that was only a copy of the
true one; he entered heaven itself . . . [not to] offer
himself again and again, the way the high priest
enters the Most Holy Place every year with blood
that is not his own . . . [Christ] has appeared once
for all at the end of the ages to do away with sin
by the sacrifice of himself' (Hebrews 9:24–26). He
is both the priest and the offering, dying in our
place as our atoning sacrifice upon the cross. But
this Saviour who died at Calvary rose again, and
as the priest-sovereign he ascended to the throne
of the universe. The God-man, Jesus, is in the glory
of heaven, triumphant, reigning and interceding for
his people (see 1 John 2:1–2). He is Melchizedek's
heir, first king of righteousness, then king of peace
(Hebrews 7:2). For Melchizedek teaches us and
Christ exemplifies that there can be no peace except
on a basis of righteousness. It was only because the
Lord Jesus was utterly righteous (sinless) that he
could be our peace, carrying in his own body the
just penalty of our sins which is demanded by God's
holy law. Christians are those who receive the
benefits of that atoning death and submit to his
sovereign authority in their lives. Like Abram, they
find themselves at the feet of their king of

righteousness and peace.

Abram received bread and wine. He must have been weary returning from the chase, and God knew that an even greater battle awaited him with the king of Sodom, so he sent his priest-king to refresh a tired and vulnerable servant. With the Melchizedek link we can see in this a wonderful picture of Christ's work in and for us. There is always refreshment in his coming. When we are weary and tempted, he comes to strengthen us. The bread and wine may express his self-giving on the cross, from which all our spiritual health and strength flow. And every time we partake of bread and wine in remembrance of him, as we feed on him in our hearts by faith, with thanksgiving, he graciously refreshes, renews and blesses us. And what greater refreshment could there be than a deeper understanding of God himself? Here, for the first time, the title 'God Most High' (*El Elyōn*) is used. God is revealed as possessor of heaven and earth, the creator, owner and ruler of everything. This is Abram's God who gave him this great victory. When you have raised your hand to him in faith and submission you will not easily be side-tracked by Sodom's offers. 'Abram gave him a tenth of everything.' He was expressing the dedication of everything he had, or was, to God Most High. It did not belong to Abram or to the king of Sodom, but to the Lord – and Abram offered it back to him in his tithe. To know that everything we have is in God's hands is the most liberating awareness. To know that it all belongs to him and comes from him and so we can put it all back into his hands, nail-pierced now; that is the key that opens the door to victory over temptation, to a deepening relationship with our king-priest, God

Most High, and to his blessing in the midst of our battles. Abram gave him, in symbol, everything. So must we.

## Chapter five

# Learning to trust more fully

*After this, the word of the LORD came to Abram in a vision:*

> *'Do not be afraid, Abram.*
> *I am your shield,*
> *your very great reward.'*

*But Abram said, 'O Sovereign LORD, what can you give me since I remain childless and the one who will inherit my estate is Eliezer of Damascus?' And Abram said, 'You have given me no children; so a servant in my household will be my heir.'*

*Then the word of the LORD came to him: 'This man will not be your heir, but a son coming from your own body will be your heir.' He took him outside and said, 'Look up at the heavens and count the stars – if indeed you can count them.' Then he said to him, 'So shall your offspring be.'*

*Abram believed the LORD, and he credited it to him as righteousness (Genesis 15:1–6).*

The Bible is a unity. Written over the centuries by many human authors, it progressively reveals the principles on which God deals with mankind. What we are learning from Abram's story is as relevant to our life today as it was to his. The reason is very simple. God's nature is unchanging. He always acts in a way that is consistent with his eternal character and attributes. Human nature is still sinful, with the same problems, the same spiritual needs. The circumstances of life today are vastly different on the surface, but underneath we are just like Abram and his contemporaries in our essential humanity. If Abram believed the Lord, so can we. If his faith was 'credited to him as righteousness', so can ours be.

## Facing up to fear

God comes to Abram in a vision to talk about his fears. Perhaps he was wondering what the outcome of his victory over Kedorlaomer would be. He might have to face reprisals and revenge from that powerful chieftain. Or, how would the king of Sodom react to Abram's refusal to take any of the goods he had recovered for himself? It is often after a victory has been won that we are attacked by fears about its implications for our future. But when we are in need like that, the God of covenant promises and faithfulness loves to meet us. And he does so by speaking to our minds about himself. That is the only way to get a grip on our tyrannizing emotions. We have to apply all that we already know about God to all that we do not and cannot know about the future. So, to the man who has very little with which to defend himself, God comes and says, 'I am your shield. You don't have to worry about your future safety, Abram, because I am not going to let you down or give you up.'

There was a deeper fear lurking in Abram's mind

and heart. It was over ten years now since first he had come to this land of promise, and although God had greatly blessed him in it, he still did not own a square metre of it and, even more important, there was still no sign of the child he had been promised as his heir. It is one thing to know and believe that God is unchanging, our shield and our very great reward, and that all we shall ever really need is in God alone. But it is another to apply that knowledge to all the frustrations and difficulties of life when specific promises seem to go unfulfilled. The answer for the person who is learning to trust God more fully is not to bottle up doubts and resentments, but honestly and directly to bring them to God. That is what Abram did. He articulated his secret fears and the way in which he had been trying to work out how the promises could possibly be fulfilled.

The conclusion that God must mean him to make his servant Eliezer his heir would have been a perfectly natural one for Abram. Cuneiform tablets discovered at Nuzi in Mesopotamia and also at Ur have shed more light on the accepted social customs of Abram's day, whereby a childless couple might legally adopt one of their servants to become their heir. Abram was simply following the natural reasoning which came to him from his social environment. 'You have given me no children; so a servant . . . will be my heir' (verse 3). What he was failing to reckon on was that the delay – as he saw it – was part of the fulfilment. He was becoming resentful of the way in which he thought God would make good his promise, and yet he had it all wrong.

The eventual birth of Isaac presented not the slightest difficulty to God. It was never in doubt. So, why the delay? Surely it was to provide the opportunity for faith to grow. If there were never any difficulties we would never need to have faith, which, in essence, is trusting in who God is and what he has said in spite of all indications to the contrary. If Sarai had been a young woman of normal child-bearing age, the problem would not have arisen. But neither would the faith! That is why God chose a man in his eighties and a barren wife to be the parents of his covenant nation. 'And so from this one man, and he as good as dead, came descendants, as numerous as the stars in the sky and as countless as the sand on the seashore' (Hebrews 11:12).

We all make Abram's mistake. We all imagine that we can make natural human projections and judgments on what we can see. We act as though we are in charge of the world, as though the timing and outworking of God's will depends upon us and not on him. But do we also follow Abram's example and pour out our doubts and inadequate analysis to God? He answers prayers like that by shining his perfect light more clearly.

Abram's suggestion of Eliezer is abruptly dismissed by the Lord and he is sent out of his tent to gaze into the night sky. As he looks at the stars, the heavens become a sort of visible word from God to him, a focus for his faith, a moment he will never forget, when God says to him, 'I am going to do what I have promised.' The stars were proof of the creative power of Yahweh, so God took him from contemplation of his own problem to the greater revelation of the divine resources. If God could hold the numberless stars in their places, he could produce a son for Abram and Sarai, and through that son, a great nation. If you want to renew your faith, look at the manifestations all around us of God's power; don't just resort to your own limited human expectations.

The way through the frustrations is always faith. 'Abram believed the LORD, and he credited it to him as righteousness' (15:6). Abram was able to live in a right relationship with God because of his faith in God's gracious character revealed in his words. He wasn't brought into this right relationship because of what he did, nor because of what was done to him, any more than today we can become Christians by doing religious things or by going through religious rituals such as baptism or confirmation, receiving Communion or joining a church. A person is made right with God through faith alone, by God's grace. Moreover, the faith which Abram exercised was not merely a belief *in* God. We are not made right with God by believing in him. 'You believe that there is one God. Good! Even the demons believe that – and shudder' (James 2:19). The western world is populated by millions of 'Christians' who say they believe in God and yet who are not the slightest bit interested in him and have no personal relationship with him whatsoever. They are what the Roman Catholic Prelate of Vienna, J. O. Meyer, recently termed 'baptized pagans'. Giving intellectual assent to a deity is not believing God. Abram's justifying faith had as its object God's promise, revealed fully in God's good time in the person of his Son, the Lord Jesus Christ. 'He was delivered over to death for our sins and was raised to life for our justification' (Romans 4:25). So as we personally exercise faith in the death of Christ to be the atoning sacrifice for our sins, and as we submit to the risen Jesus, acknowledging him to be our Lord, we too can know that we have been made right with God because of his free grace and mercy, received by faith.

That is the beginning, but it is also the essential characteristic of all that will follow. The Christian lives a life of faith. Often the pathway twists and turns; it certainly is not easy going. It would be another fifteen years after this incident before Isaac was born. But they were not wasted years, for God was building Abram into a giant of faith through all the trials and tests that awaited him. They were, to use Oswald Sanders' phrase, 'God's votes of confidence' in his man. Abram went on believing, although everything seemed against the birth of a child to this ageing couple. All the evidence and arguments were against it, but God had spoken and that settled it for Abram, as it should do for us.

\*     \*     \*

*He also said to him, 'I am the LORD, who brought you out of Ur of the Chaldeans to give you this land to take possession of it.'*

*But Abram said, 'O Sovereign LORD, how can I know that I shall gain possession of it?'*

*So the LORD said to him, 'Bring me a heifer, a goat and a ram, each three years old, along with a dove and a young pigeon.'*

*Abram brought all these to him, cut them in two and arranged the halves opposite each other; the birds, however, he did not cut in half. Then birds of prey came down on the carcasses, but Abram drove them away.*

*As the sun was setting, Abram fell into a deep sleep, and a thick and dreadful darkness came over him. Then the LORD said to him, 'Know for certain that your descendants will be strangers in a country not their own, and they will be enslaved and ill-treated four hundred years. But I will punish the nation they serve as slaves, and afterwards they will come out with great possessions. You, however, will go to your fathers in peace and be buried at a good old age. In the fourth generation your descendants will come back here, for the sin of the Amorites has not yet reached its full measure.'*

*When the sun had set and darkness had fallen, a smoking fire pot with a blazing torch appeared and passed between the pieces. On that day the LORD made a covenant with Abram and said, 'To your descendants I give this land, from the river of Egypt to the great river, the Euphrates'* (Genesis 15:7–18).

## Confirming the commitment

Having dealt with the problem of the son, God now turns to the other strand of the covenant promise, as yet equally unfulfilled: 'to give you this land'. It is all too easy to pass over God's declaration, 'I am the LORD', as though it were simply a note of who is speaking. Impatiently we say, 'Of course Abram knew the LORD had brought him out of Ur – why say that again?', and rush on to the next verse. We are not reading the Bible with Bible eyes! Actually, we are being taught one of the most significant lessons in the school of faith – that faith is only strong insofar as it is a response to the character of God. And it is through God's names that his nature is revealed. So whenever we come across the divine name of the LORD, in capital letters in an English version and usually transliterated Yahweh (Jehovah), we must build into that the central revelation of the eternal faithfulness of God seen in his covenant grace and mercy to his people. He is the God who makes and keeps his promises. Therefore he is the God who can be, above everything, trusted, rested in and relied upon to keep his word. Abram is being reminded that this is the God who brought him from Ur. He is not a God to guide his people into cul-de-sacs, nor to mislead those who trust him. If his purpose in bringing Abram out of Ur was to give him this land, then he will do it.

As God renews his promise to Abram, there begins a dialogue of faith. Again Abram opens his heart to God and expresses his deep questioning: 'How can I *know* I shall possess it?' His faith was struggling with its doubts and queries. It wanted to be stronger, to be certain, which is a mark of its authenticity. Believing God is not a matter of unquestioning acceptance, but of bringing our problems honestly to him. There is a distorted view, sometimes held by insecure Christians, which says that real faith puts an end to all questioning. I remember once meeting a girl student who was facing doubts and problems, both intellectually and personally, in her Christian discipleship. She had been told by a well-meaning but unwise counsellor that as Jesus had told those whose eyes offended to pluck them out, or whose hand had offended to cut it off, in her case her mind was the offender, so she had to stop thinking and simply relax into the love of Jesus. As a Christian magazine article put it, that is tantamount to saying, 'Jesus wants me for a zombie!' Faith never grows by short-circuiting the mind. It grows by bringing our questions honestly to God and asking him to apply his self-revelation in Scripture to our current problems, by his Spirit. There are times when we long for some more tangible evidence of God's dealing with us and when we need to pour out our thoughts to God. 'Lord, how can I know?' I believe God loves to answer honest prayers like that. No rebuke was given to Abram, but rather a gracious answer to his specific problem.

At first glance, God's response seems difficult to grasp. Abram is required to bring together 'a heifer, a goat and a ram, each three years old, along with a dove and a young pigeon', to cut the animals in two and arrange the halves opposite each other. To us this may seem strange, but Abram knew exactly what he was doing. He knew from his childhood in Chaldea that this was how you drew up a solemn, binding agreement. At a time when written agreements were comparatively rare, though certainly not unknown, this was the equivalent of a legal document, as archaeological evidence has shown. God required Abram to take one of each species of animal later to be designated in the law as suitable for sacrifice. As in the sacrificial ritual, the animals are divided but the birds are not, and between them there is a space that becomes a path. It is interesting that many of the Near Eastern peoples talked about 'cutting' a covenant. The idea was that the animals were cut in two, divided, and a way through the middle made, so that the two parties who were concluding the agreement identified with each other as they each walked through the middle. The divided animals denoted the two parties and the walking between the pieces symbolized their unity in the covenant being made. It is also probable that the cutting up of the animals was a ritual enactment of a covenant meal, by which the agreement between the parties was sealed and ratified.

So God in his grace is coming to Abram where

he is, taking something he does understand in order to help him cope with what he does not understand. That is characteristic of grace. The heart of the Christian faith lies not in abstract theological propositions or philosophical theories but in a human life, a human death and a human resurrection. God communicates in terms that are universally comprehensible. But again in the story there is delay. The covenant ceremony is prepared early in the morning and then Abram was to wait for God to come to ratify it. The man of faith spent the day driving off the birds of prey that came to devour the meat. Just imagine that long, hot day and how often he had to get up and do it again as the vultures circled round and round in the blue sky above him. All day long waiting for God. Don't you think he sometimes wondered if he'd heard God correctly; if he had got it right? But the waiting is all part of God's answer to the question 'How can I *know*?' There was nothing Abram could do but be obedient, wait for God and show his obedience by defending the sacrifices on which the covenant ceremony depended. His part was to be faithful and to see that what God had commanded was there ready for him. The lesson he was learning is that we often come to trust God more fully and to be more sure of him by waiting. That is how he 'stretches' our faith. Every time a vulture swooped down out of the sky, Abram's faith was tested. Am I going to let it settle and destroy what God has asked me to provide, or am I going to believe God and go on waiting, however long it may be? That is the test that every Christian faces at some time or other.

The day draws to its end and the sun is setting. Night will suddenly descend. And there is a worn-out, puzzled Abram who falls into a deep sleep, but it is more than an ordinary sleep as this is more than an ordinary nightfall. There fell on Abram 'a thick and dreadful darkness' (verse 12), because the vision God was about to grant him was of a dark and dreadful period of suffering for his promised descendants. In answer to his question 'How can I know that I shall gain possession of the land?', God opens the door of the future and reveals to Abram that his descendants will face four centuries of life in an alien country, culminating in oppression and slavery. The reference is of course to their entry into Egypt under Jacob, which period ended with the exodus under Moses 430 years later (Exodus 12:40–41). God tells Abram of the punishments which will come on their oppressors, punishments which we know as the plagues (Exodus 7–11). The plague that finally devastated Egypt was the occasion of the passover by which Israel was redeemed (Exodus 12), and the whole nation came out, as God foretold, with great spoil from the Egyptians, who could not get rid of them quickly enough (Exodus 12:36). Abram will not see this, God tells him, since it will be four 'generations' before his descendants return. In fact it was to be 400 years; but the word usually translated 'generation' can mean a longer time-span such as a century. God explains the reason for the delay: 'the sin of the Amorites has not yet reached its full measure' (verse 16b).

This is a very significant statement indeed. The Amorites, the most powerful of the Canaanite tribes, are representative of all the inhabitants of the land promised to Abram. They would eventually fall when the Israelites invaded and conquered Canaan under Joshua's leadership. The slaughter that this involved is often used as an argument against the love and justice of God, misrepresenting him as the slaughterer of innocent people. But this statement indicates God's character as well as explaining God's delay. He was waiting in grace for 400 years. It was only when Canaanite morality had sunk irretrievably, beyond all reformation, that God acted in judgment against them, to take the land from them and give it to those who might hold it more worthily. The conquest of the land under Joshua was an act of God's justice, for which the Israelites had endured four centuries of hardship until it was morally right for God to act in judgment. For us, an important lesson in this is that when God seems to delay, it is because more things are happening than we can see. God has his perfect timing and none of the waiting is longer than it need be. It is often through the horror of the darkness that we learn really to trust God's infallible wisdom. Jesus went out into the darkness of separation from the Father so that his light and love might enter our lives. So whatever night we may be called to go through, as we learn to trust him in the dark we know that resurrection light will ultimately be ours. In the words of Isaiah: 'Let him who walks in the dark, who has no light, trust in the name of the LORD and rely on his God' (Isaiah 50:10).

At last God came to Abram and ratified his covenant. 'A smoking fire pot with a blazing torch appeared and passed between the pieces' (15:17). God came to the man who waited in faith, and when he came he manifested his glory. Smoke and fire are the characteristic symbols of God's presence in the Old Testament. It was to be so at Mount Sinai when he came down to reveal himself in the law. It was to be so throughout the exodus period, in the pillar of cloud and the pillar of fire. So here, with great solemnity, the Lord passes between the pieces Abram has prepared and preserved, in an unforgettable ratification of his covenant promise. There is no record of Abram walking between the pieces since God's covenant is not a bargain between equals. It is totally dependent on the divine initiative of grace, establishing the fellowship-relationship purely because he wills it. The man of faith contributes nothing. His role is to receive what God gives, obey what God commands and so live in the enjoyment of God's blessings.

With God's visible action came the strengthening word, a renewed word of promise about the land given in greater detail than ever before, 'from the river of Egypt to the great river Euphrates' (15:18b). That promise was literally fulfilled, but only during the reign of King David and for a short time under his son Solomon (see 2 Chronicles 8:7–8). To Abram's spiritual descendants, however, the kingdom of great David's greater Son has spread throughout the earth. That should encourage us when it seems as though we are in the dark, not understanding why we have to wait for God's promises to be fulfilled. That is precisely the moment for faith to hold on to God's Word and to say, 'I know that the God who has brought me to this point is not going to let me down now, so I am going to confirm my commitment to him, whatever the appearances may be, because he is committed to me for ever.'

## *Chapter six*

# A tragic mistake

*Now Sarai, Abram's wife, had borne him no children. But she had an Egyptian maidservant named Hagar; so she said to Abram, 'The LORD has kept me from having children. Go, sleep with my maidservant; perhaps I can build a family through her.'*

*Abram agreed to what Sarai said. So after Abram had been living in Canaan ten years, Sarai his wife took her Egyptian maidservant Hagar and gave her to her husband to be his wife. He slept with Hagar, and she conceived.*

*When she knew she was pregnant, she began to despise her mistress. Then Sarai said to Abram, 'You are responsible for the wrong I am suffering. I put my servant in your arms, and now that she knows she is pregnant, she despises me. May the LORD judge between you and me.'*

*'Your servant is in your hands,' Abram said. 'Do with her whatever you think best.' Then Sarai ill-treated Hagar; so she fled from her.*

*The angel of the LORD found Hagar near a spring in the desert; it was the spring that is beside the road to Shur. And he said, 'Hagar, servant of Sarai, where have you come from, and where are you going?'*

'I'm running away from my mistress Sarai,' she answered.

Then the angel of the LORD told her, 'Go back to your mistress and submit to her.' The angel added, 'I will so increase your descendants that they will be too numerous to count.'

The angel of the LORD also said to her:

> 'You are now with child
> and you will have a son.
> You shall name him Ishmael,
> for the LORD has heard of
> your misery.
> He will be a wild donkey of a
> man;
> his hand will be against
> everyone
> and everyone's hand against
> him,
> and he will live in hostility
> towards all his brothers.'

She gave this name to the LORD who spoke to her: 'You are the God who sees me,' for she said, 'I have now seen the One who sees me.' That is why the well was called Beer Lahai Roi; it is still there, between Kadesh and Bered.

So Hagar bore Abram a son, and Abram gave the name Ishmael to the son she had borne. Abram was eighty-six years old when Hagar bore him Ishmael (Genesis 16:1–16).


'Roller-coaster Christianity' is a phenomenon with which we are all very familiar. The Christian life becomes a series of long, slow hauls and violent plunges; a switch-back existence which has its moments of exhilaration, but if persisted in for too long does terrible things to your internal equilibrium. There are times in Abram's story when the man who believed God doesn't! We might be tempted to think the contrasts overdrawn if we did not look into our own hearts and see the same sort of contradictions, however much we seek to follow the Lord.

## The roots of the problem

We are back with the problem of childlessness, but this time we see it from Sarai's viewpoint. They had been living in the land for ten years, but as yet there was no sign of a son and heir. You can imagine how this began to dominate Sarai's thinking, since all the future purposes for which they had launched into this adventure into the unknown depended on the birth of the child. Sarai was barren. She saw herself as responsible, and so she began to turn over in her mind what she could do about it. We must not forget that she had not experienced the revelations God had given to her husband. She knew what Yahweh had promised Abram and she knew that he was to be trusted, but she had not had Abram's privileged personal relationship with the LORD. So she tended to judge the situation more by her own reasoning than by faith. Not unnaturally, Sarai was inclined to look at things from a human standpoint and to work out solutions for herself. When she said to Abram, 'The LORD has kept me from having children' (verse 2), she was right. He was timing the whole story according to a master plan that would see Isaac born at exactly the right moment. But Sarai's deduction that Abram should sleep with her Egyptian maid Hagar was all wrong. 'Perhaps I can build a family through her,' she said (verse 2). That is putting all the onus for the fulfilment of the promise on Sarai rather than on God. No wonder she felt under such pressure. It would run through her mind over and over again: 'When is this promise going to be fulfilled? What is wrong with me that God has not fulfilled it? How can he through me, anyway, as I am barren?' Her tragic mistake was to take matters into her own hands.

Just as Abram's previous suggestion to God that Eliezer would have to be his heir was a product of the culture he came from, so was Sarai's suggestion to Abram about Hagar. The Nuzi tablets from Mesopotamia tell us that if a wife was unable to have a child, she could choose to give her maid to her husband, so that she might produce the heir for her. The child would be legally recognized as the couple's child and heir unless and until they subsequently had a child of their own, who would then necessarily displace any servant or maid's son. After all, God had said the son would come from Abram's body (15:4), not hers, Sarai might have reasoned. They had better do what they could. The child must come through Hagar. Thinking it through and responding to cultural pressures coupled with lack of faith, Sarai began to usurp the providence of God, and whenever that happens the result is always tragic.

'Abram agreed to what Sarai said' (verse 2b). He of all people should have known better. He should have applied the revelation of God which he had received and told Sarai she was wrong. It is difficult for us to know what Abram's view about monogamous marriage would have been at this time. The text at this point contains no hint about it and it is certainly true to say that in other respects God deals with the patriarchs in terms of the culture of their time. So he allows them to do things which will later be forbidden in the legislation given through Moses. Thus Abraham will plant a tree in Genesis 21:33 where 'he called upon the name of the LORD', which is forbidden in Deuteronomy 16:21, as is the erection of a 'sacred stone' in the next verse, although Jacob sets up a stone on a pillar in Genesis 28:18. It may be that marriage to more than one wife was permitted until the Mosaic era, especially if this was seen as the answer to barrenness. Indeed, if we think of the birth of Samuel to the previously barren Hannah (1 Samuel 1:1–20), it seems that the practice may have continued even after Moses. Much will depend on when the principle of Genesis 2:24 was first enunciated: 'For this reason a man will leave his father and mother and be united to his wife, and they will become one flesh'. Jesus clearly taught this statement as the direct word of God, linking it with the creation of man and woman (Matthew 19:4–5). But was the statement given at the beginning, or later revealed as the divine word through Moses when the book of Genesis was written? As Abram walked with God, did he learn what God's principles for human relationships were? Whatever the answers to these difficult questions may be, it is clear that Abram was wrong to entertain Sarai's suggestion of this strategy as a way to provide the promised heir. The primary reason is that it was a human expedient which did not depend on faith at all.

Abram's basic mistake was to begin to meddle with what God had already said and to find a way round it on the grounds of exceptional circumstances. It all sounded so reasonable, but it is the way tragic mistakes are still made. At root, it indicates a rejection of the sufficiency of God's truth to guide us and therefore of its authority. Take, for example, some of the medical-ethical questions of our contemporary debates. This is how the argument runs. With the amazing capabilities now in the hands of genetic engineers, unimagined fifty years ago, let alone in Bible times, we cannot of course expect the Bible to have anything specific to say to help us. We don't look there for guidance, we have to work out something suitable for ourselves. Our circumstances are so different today that God's Word either has nothing to say or has to be radically reinterpreted to be acceptable to our enlightened thinking. That argument is everywhere today. When it appeals to our natural desire to be happy and seems to overcome fear and distrust, it is very hard to answer. When it is presented by someone we love, someone like Sarai who was apparently willing to make a great personal sacrifice in order to give her husband what he most wanted, it is almost impossible to resist. 'Abram agreed to what Sarai said', guided by her arguments rather than God's promise. But what seemed so right was actually so tragically wrong. 'Everything that does not come from faith is sin' (Romans 14:23).

## Sin pays its wage

Hagar was one of the slaves Abram had brought with him out of Egypt, probably one of the Pharaoh's gifts. Although that episode of failure was forgiven, it is instructive to see how its consequences provided an ingredient in this new mistake. As soon as Hagar was known to be pregnant, the whole situation took a downward turn. One sin always leads to another. In Hagar it led to the sin of pride. She would produce the heir which her mistress could not, and so she began to hold Sarai in contempt and to despise her. In Sarai it produced the sin of jealousy, which led her to blame Abram for what had happened. In one sense it was blame rightly apportioned, but clearly their relationship was soured. We take a step away from God and we always begin to find fault and quarrel with others. We do not blame ourselves; we reproach others for their faults. So many marriages are poisoned by just this mechanism. Sarai became a cauldron of wounded pride and seething jealousy, which turned into hatred and malice towards this slave girl. Here we see the classic triangle situation at work, a powerful reminder of the perilous course we embark upon whenever we decide to trust ourselves rather than God. In Abram it produced the sin of withdrawal from responsibility, a false neutrality that only wanted to wash his hands of the whole situation, a callous indifference that was prepared to leave Hagar to her fate. 'She's your servant,' he told his wife. 'Do whatever you like with her.' Anything for a quiet life! It seems to be a particularly masculine sin.

Then Sarai launched a counter-attack of such bitterness against Hagar that she fled. This is the fruit of human wisdom and the self-confident tragic mistake when Christians manipulate and manoeuvre circumstances in order to get themselves into positions God never meant them to have. The result is always sorrow, just as it is with those who try to dominate and control the lives of others by unfair pressures to get their own way, irrespective of God's will. We need to take a long, hard look at the consequences when we are tempted to go our own way, to realize the multiplication effect of sin, when we argue ourselves into stepping around God's commandments.

## God to the rescue

Yet in all this confusion and distress God was also involved. Sarai might have imagined that she had got rid of Hagar relatively easily, but the knock-on effects of sin are not so lightly dismissed. The God who sees (verse 13) was going to restore Hagar and her son to Sarai's household for many years to come. The repercussions of our folly may dog our footsteps for a long time. Naturally Hagar set off for home in Egypt. She was on the road to Shur, on the north-east Egyptian frontier. But there, in the desert, God caught up with her (verse 7). He came in the form of an angel, but the fact that she gave the angel a divine name ('The One who sees') has encouraged many Bible students to suggest that this visitation may in fact have been a pre-incarnational appearance of the Lord Jesus Christ himself. Certainly this was God coming to meet a proud, bitter woman, who was in many ways more sinned against than sinning, at the point of her need.

He begins by showing her that she cannot run away. She is united with Abram, so she must return and submit to Sarai. It's always tempting to want to run away from our past mistakes and failures, but we cannot evade God's grasp. Running away is never the answer to complex personal problems. The way out of them is back. The way to win is to submit. For Hagar that would be very hard, but God gave her a promise to encourage her on the path of obedience – her son, to be called Ishmael ('God hears'), will also be the father of a multitude. If she has been evicted by Sarai and kicked around all her life because she is a slave girl, then God affirms that no-one will push Ishmael around. 'He will be a wild donkey of a man', always at variance with his brothers, always hostile. That is how sin multiplies.

But where sin increases, grace increases all the more (Romans 5:20). God is not remote and unmoved by our tragic errors or foolish rebellions. He reveals himself to a pagan slave girl like Hagar because he is the God who sees, and in his seeing he cares and loves and intervenes, just as in his hearing prayer he answers. He defends the helpless and meets them in their troubles. Unlike her Egyptian idols with their carved eyes which cannot see a thing, the living God sees everything. 'You are a God of seeing,' Hagar confesses, 'and I have seen the God who sees me.' We should never imagine that we are beyond his grasp, however tragic our experiences may have been. But his rescue mission will involve us in going back with him to unscramble what has gone wrong, to submit to his authority in the very place where before we left his pathway.

Hagar did return and events took their natural course. That is how God has ordained life should be. Cause and effect follow a regular pattern and divine intervention to prevent it is a very rare occurrence. Hagar's son was born and Abram had to cope with the two wives, with Sarai's jealousy and Hagar's pride. He had to cope with Ishmael, the wild donkey, growing up in his household – a son, but not the son of the promise. Sarai had to cope with the perpetual rebuke to her barrenness of Hagar's son growing up. Hagar had to cope with the lash of her mistress's tongue and her invariable hostility as she went back and submitted. Did God not care? Of course he did. He cares and forgives, but he does not necessarily remove the consequences of our sins. That is why it is so important that we should walk closely with him. He will give grace to cope with those consequences but he does not lift us out of them as if they had never happened. That would not help us to trust and obey him. And remember, that is the greatest good for which he is working in our lives.

## Chapter seven

# A changed man

*When Abram was ninety-nine years old, the LORD
appeared to him and said, 'I am God Almighty;
walk before me and be blameless. I will confirm
my covenant between me and you and will greatly
increase your numbers.'*

*Abram fell face down, and God said to him, 'As
for me, this is my covenant with you: You will be
the father of many nations. No longer will you be
called Abram; your name will be Abraham, for I
have made you a father of many nations. I will make
you very fruitful; I will make nations of you, and
kings will come from you. I will establish my
covenant as an everlasting covenant between me and
you and your descendants after you for the generations to come, to be your God and the God of your
descendants after you. The whole land of Canaan,
where you are now an alien, I will give as an everlasting possession to you and your descendants after
you; and I will be their God.'*

*Then God said to Abraham, 'As for you, you
must keep my covenant, you and your descendants
after you for the generations to come. This is my
covenant with you and your descendants after you,
the covenant you are to keep: Every male among*

*you shall be circumcised. You are to undergo circumcision, and it will be the sign of the covenant between me and you. For the generations to come every male among you who is eight days old must be circumcised, including those born in your household or bought with money from a foreigner – those who are not your offspring. Whether born in your household or bought with your money, they must be circumcised. My covenant in your flesh is to be an everlasting covenant. Any uncircumcised male, who has not been circumcised in the flesh, will be cut off from his people; he has broken my covenant'* (Genesis 17:1–14).

Reading the story of Abram through at a sitting, we might easily form the impression that his life was crowded with revelations of God and we might be tempted to envy him. How much easier the life of faith would be if only God appeared to me in visions, or if I could actually hear his voice! But is that really true? Jesus told Thomas, 'Because you have seen me, you have believed; blessed are those who have not seen and yet have believed' (John 20:29). For while we have been brought up on the view that seeing is believing, the Lord teaches his church that believing is seeing. Nor was Abram continually blitzed with sensory evidence of God's reality! Between his departure from Haran, aged seventy-five, and the start of chapter 17, twenty-four years have passed. In that time we are told that God spoke to him at Bethel, on entering the land. God met with him again after Lot's departure, and the third and last encounter with God was in the renewal of the covenant promises, after his victory over Kedorlaomer and his allies. Three recorded meetings with God hardly constitute a revelation around every corner! Moreover, they all occurred before Ishmael was born, and thirteen years have passed since that event. Between chapters 16 and 17 of Genesis lie thirteen years of silence in which nothing spectacular seems to have happened, nothing that the Holy Spirit wanted to record as he inspired the writing of Abram's story. They were thirteen years in which Abram was left to walk by faith while the child of the promise remained unborn and while he still owned none of the land which God had designated his. They were years in which his helplessness to do anything about the situation, his own utter inability, were indelibly imprinted on his thinking day after day. And then suddenly, in his one hundredth year, the Lord of the covenant reveals himself again to his servant, just at the point of his most acute need, to meet it perfectly and to move his purposes a great step forward.

Special manifestations of God are always for special purposes. They come because God wills them, not because we want them or work them up. Yet there are Christians who are always on the look-out for the special, the overwhelming, the spectacular in their experience, without which they become very discouraged. What happens is that their Christian lives become an intense straining after some new and startling evidence of the presence of God, or some special awareness of his love. God speaking through the Bible and our response in prayer is too predictable, too ordinary for them. Of course those things can become dry and routine if we do not walk humbly with our God and if we allow sin to build barriers between us and him. Often the 'special' experiences we focus on, and even boast about, are God in his grace reaching out to us in our need, when our faith has reached a low ebb, or when we have tolerated sin in our lives. They are emergency rescues which are usually dramatic, but they are hardly experiences that do us any credit. And yet in some circles, unless these upheavals occur with increasing regularity and even intensity, it will be questioned whether you are really going on with God at all. But anyone who has been a Christian for a number of years and sought to live a consistent Christian life in God's strength, knows that there are miles of the journey when we have to walk on, by faith, without any special excitements or vivid experiences. That is the way we are taught to trust in God, not ourselves. It is in the ordinary routine periods that God nurtures within us a faith that is independent of both our feelings and our circumstances, but which is rooted in the living God who does not change and who will always keep his word. Thank God for every new experience of his grace we receive, for the highlights and mountain peaks of our Christian lives, but let us remember that the heart of our Christianity is in our everyday walk with God, as we learn to go on, trusting where we cannot see.

## The covenant pattern

The making of a treaty, or covenant, was a familiar practice among the people of the ancient Near East. They were especially used to establishing the relationship between a conqueror (the lord) and his vassal (the servant). Obviously, the terms of the treaty would be unilaterally enforced by the victor. All treaties followed a similar pattern. At the beginning the great king would be introduced by name, with his full titles, and then the historical reasons for the treaty would be described. After this, the stipulations of the treaty would follow, typically requiring loyalty to the lord and payment of tribute. Then there would be a list of witnesses, including the gods and natural phenomena, and the treaty would conclude with the curses which would be invoked if its terms were broken and the blessings which would accrue with its keeping. Many historical examples also exist of covenants or treaties between a god and a king. Since this was such a familiar pattern, Yahweh clearly chose to use it to teach Abram here, and later the whole nation of Israel, what the relationship with himself, which he had brought them into, involved, and what God required of his people.

As we follow through this confirmation of the covenant, we shall find some of the ingredients mentioned above forming the structure of what the Lord said and did. First, God comes on his own initiative to Abram, revealing his character and attributes in a new name (*El Shaddai*) which both demands Abram's obedience and promises his blessing. Once again, command and promise are yoked together. Abram's response is to prostrate himself before the Lord. God then gives Abram a new name and develops more fully than ever before the promises he is making to him and his descendants. These in turn are followed by the covenant obligations or requirements, which focus on circumcision as the covenant sign. The promises (verses 4–8) are introduced by the key phrase on the lips of God, 'As for me . . .'; the obligations (verses 9–14) are introduced by the equivalent, 'As for you . . .'.

What we must firmly grasp is that the covenant

94

is not a bargain struck between equals. God does not come to Abram to say, 'Now if you do this for me, I'll do this for you.' The covenant is imposed by God on the man of faith. At its heart lies the relationship, expressed later in Exodus 6:7, 'I will be your God and you will be my people.' There is no option, no alternative to this action of God's grace. Abram's role is not to sign his name in agreement so much as to fall on his face in worship. The requirements are all going to be on the part of the master. He is going to dictate the path his people will follow, but the fact that he does that is the mark of his grace. It is because God desires to bless us that he places covenant obligations, which are always for our good, upon us. Again we need to be precise and careful in our thinking here. We can so easily distort God's grace into a reward for our works. But grace is mercy and favour that we do not and cannot merit, much less earn. Grace gives us what we do not deserve (mercy and forgiveness) in the place of what we do (condemnation and judgment). So when God comes to Abram he is not saying, 'If you walk before me and live a blameless life, I will condescend to be your God.' If that were so, we would be locked into a religion of works, by which we might attempt to make ourselves good enough for God. That is the essence of all man-made religions, but it is totally contradicted by the Bible's teaching that a man can only be made right with God by grace, through faith (see *e.g.* Ephesians 2:1–10). No, God is saying to Abram (and to us, his spiritual descendants), 'I am calling you into a personal relationship with me, which I have elected to bring you into, and you will enter fully into its blessing as you walk with me in loyalty and love.'

In the ancient Near-Eastern treaties the names of the two parties concerned were very important. Indeed, one can see the same pattern in our royal charters and commissions to this very day. God revealed himself with a new name, *El Shaddai*, 'God Almighty' (17:1). He also gave a new name to his servant. 'No longer will you be called Abram; your name will be Abraham' (verse 5). The title *El Shaddai* is used on several occasions in the book of Genesis, particularly in the life of Jacob and always in the context of God's faithfulness in fulfilling his covenant promises (see 28:3; 35:11; 48:3; 49:25). Some scholars suggest that at root the word means 'God the mountain', or 'the immovable rock', and so it speaks of his unchanging stability together with his strength and power to keep and honour his word. Certainly the way it is used underlines the ability of God to change situations that, humanly speaking, are hopeless. That is why it is so appropriate at the end of Abram's thirteen childless, hopeless years that God reveals himself in these terms. When we are at the end of our tether we need to remember that at the other end is *El Shaddai*.

But he makes demands. 'Walk before me and be blameless' (verse 1). Some people are inclined to interpret this as meaning 'sinless', but the word really means 'whole-hearted', fully committed. This is a quality which is specially dear to God, because it involves putting him first, living by faith, staking everything on him. That is what he always asks from his covenant people. Such obedience is the fruit of a life that is consciously aware of God's eye upon it. He knows the thoughts of our minds and the motivations of our wills. To walk blamelessly is to open up every situation of life to God for his direction and control. Obedience is the key that opens the door to the enjoyment of covenant promises.

## The covenant promises

'As for me, this is my covenant with you: You will be the father of many nations . . . I will make you very fruitful; I will make nations of you, and kings will come from you. . . . The whole land of Canaan, where you are now an alien, I will give as an everlasting possession to you and your descendants after you . . .' (verses 4, 6, 8).

There are two extra ingredients in this revelation. The first is the personal promise which is caught up in the change of name from Abram to Abraham, which God explains by saying, 'I have made you a father of many nations' (verse 5). The past tense is used, as so often in the Bible, to denote certainty. Because God has willed it, it has happened in his eyes, even though the outward fulfilment has yet to be seen on earth. So, God puts the promise into terms which Abram cannot ignore. Here at ninety-nine years of age, the man who only has one son is to be known as 'father of a multitude'. I don't think he can have found that very easy! Don't you think there would have been plenty of jokes among the Canaanites at his expense? What did he think he was doing, changing his name like that? He was believing God, because God had made him a new man.

The other new ingredient is the spelling out of the new relationship which will exist between God and Abraham's family. 'I will establish my covenant as an everlasting covenant . . . to be your God and the God of your descendants after you' (verse 7).

The 'everlasting' covenant is still in existence between God and his people. It is at the heart of what it means to become a Christian. All that God was to Abraham then, he is to every one of his people still. For the new covenant, sealed with the blood of God's own Son, the Lord Jesus Christ, is equally a covenant that depends upon God's initiative of grace. 'I will be your God.' The great difference is that the promise God made through Jeremiah has now been fulfilled, in Christ. No longer is it a covenant written on stone or parchment. 'I will put my law in their minds and write it on their hearts. I will be their God, and they will be my people' (Jeremiah 31:33). The glory of the new covenant is that the life of God is planted within the human personality of the Christian, as the Holy Spirit comes to indwell each child of God, changing us, from the inside out, to make us more and more like Christ. But we only know the riches of that potential as we give ourselves up to him, loving God with all our heart, will, mind and strength. When we cease to hold on to our lives and to demand that we belong to ourselves, when we give ourselves into God's hands, then God becomes our own possession, because we become his. When we lose ourselves in God, we find our true selves, because we have all that really matters, or lasts, in him alone.

## The covenant requirements

'As for you, you must keep my covenant' (verse 9a). That is all, but it involves an unreserved commitment to God and an unrestricted obedience to his commands. As F. D. Kidner points out: 'The striking feature of the stipulations is their lack of

98

detail. To be *committed* was all.' Such commitment was to be marked in a physical way, in Abraham and all of his descendants, by the covenant sign of circumcision. Again, this was not something new or strange to Abraham, since it was widespread practice in the Near East, usually marking the threshold of adult male life. But what was new was the early age at which it was to be administered – eight days old – and the significance which God invested in it. Circumcision was to be the mark of belonging to the people of God. That is why every male member of the covenant community, whether born as a descendant of Abraham or as a Gentile, must bear the sign or be cut off from God's people (verse 14). Just as God had invested the physical phenomenon of the rainbow with covenant significance in his dealings with Noah, as a sign that he would never flood the earth again (9:12–16), so Abraham and his descendants were to carry in their bodies the sign that they belonged to Yahweh and that they would be faithful to him. Circumcision was to be the outward mark of their inward allegiance. It was not firstly a sign of their consecration to God, however, but of his commitment in grace to them; a tangible reminder of the promises of God and of the fact that those promises all applied to the man within the covenant because God had chosen him to receive his grace. As Alec Motyer puts it, 'Covenant signs declare covenant promises to covenant people.'

And what of the members of the new covenant community, the church? The outward sign was always meaningless unless it was accompanied by obedience. The thing signified (covenant faithfulness in obedience) had to be present for the sign to have any value. So Paul affirms that circumcision is not merely outward and physical, but rather it is 'circumcision of the heart, by the Spirit, not by the written code' (Romans 2:29). But as with all the ceremonial law of the Old Testament, the symbol of circumcision found its perfect fulfilment in Christ, who was himself the perfectly obedient son of the covenant. Through the surrender of Christ's perfect sinless will in the place of my sinful, rebellious will on the cross, all that circumcision spoke of regarding total obedience to the Father's will, which I could never fulfil, Jesus met completely. So in Christ, neither circumcision nor uncircumcision has any value. 'What counts is a new creation' (Galatians 6:15b). 'The only thing that counts is faith expressing itself through love' (Galatians 5:6). The reality to which the physical rite and sign pointed is the spiritual dedication of the Christian's life in obedient discipleship. That is what Paul means when he uses the metaphor of circumcision in Colossians 2:11–12: 'In [Christ] you were also circumcised, in the putting off of the sinful nature [the flesh], not with a circumcision done by the hands of men but with the circumcision done by Christ, having been buried with him in baptism and raised with him through your faith in the power of God, who raised him from the dead.'

If there is an equivalent initiation sign on entry into the new covenant community it is, as Paul here indicates, the sign of baptism. But more important than any sacramental sign is the fact of the new relationship with God brought about through the death and resurrection of Christ. This new birth, symbolized perhaps by Abraham's new name, is known by the writing of God's covenant requirements on the hearts of his people in every generation. 'You shall keep my covenant' still holds true.

Not that we obey in order to become God's people, but that being made God's people by grace, we want to please the Father who has loved us so much and so we delight to obey him. It is the indispensable condition of fellowship with God, and there is always even more grace to enable us to obey. Those to whom God promises, he commands. Those whom he commands, he enables. Covenant privileges are dependent on covenant obligations.

## Chapter eight

# Can God do the impossible?

God also said to Abraham, 'As for Sarai your wife, you are no longer to call her Sarai; her name will be Sarah. I will bless her and will surely give you a son by her. I will bless her so that she will be the mother of nations; kings of peoples will come from her.'

Abraham fell face down; he laughed and said to himself, 'Will a son be born to a man a hundred years old? Will Sarah bear a child at the age of ninety?' And Abraham said to God, 'If only Ishmael might live under your blessing!'

Then God said, 'Yes, but your wife Sarah will bear you a son, and you will call him Isaac. I will establish my covenant with him as an everlasting covenant for his descendants after him. And as for Ishmael, I have heard you: I will surely bless him; I will make him fruitful and will greatly increase his numbers. He will be the father of twelve rulers, and I will make him into a great nation. But my covenant I will establish with Isaac, whom Sarah will bear to you by this time next year.' When he had finished speaking with Abraham, God went up from him.

On that very day Abraham took his son Ishmael and all those born in his household or bought with

*his money, every male in his household, and circum-*
*cised them, as God told him. Abraham was ninety-*
*nine years old when he was circumcised, and his*
*son Ishmael was thirteen; Abraham and his son*
*Ishmael were both circumcised on the same day.*
*And every male in Abraham's household, including*
*those born in his household or bought from a for-*
*eigner, was circumcised with him.*

*The LORD appeared to Abraham near the great*
*trees of Mamre while he was sitting at the entrance*
*to his tent in the heat of the day. Abraham looked*
*up and saw three men standing nearby. When he*
*saw them, he hurried from the entrance of his tent*
*to meet them and bowed low to the ground.*

*He said, 'If I have found favour in your eyes, my*
*lord, do not pass your servant by. Let a little water*
*be brought, and then you may all wash your feet*
*and rest under this tree. Let me get you something*
*to eat, so you can be refreshed and then go on your*
*way – now that you have come to your servant.'*

*'Very well,' they answered, 'do as you say.'*

*So Abraham hurried into the tent to Sarah.*
*'Quick,' he said, 'get three seahs of fine flour and*
*knead it and bake some bread.'*

*Then he ran to the herd and selected a choice,*
*tender calf and gave it to a servant, who hurried to*
*prepare it. He then brought some curds and milk*
*and the calf that had been prepared, and set these*
*before them. While they ate, he stood near them*
*under a tree.*

*'Where is your wife Sarah?' they asked him.*

*'There, in the tent,' he said.*

*Then the LORD said, 'I will surely return to you*
*about this time next year, and Sarah your wife will*
*have a son.'*

*Now Sarah was listening at the entrance to the*

*tent, which was behind him. Abraham and Sarah
were already old and well advanced in years, and
Sarah was past the age of childbearing. So Sarah
laughed to herself as she thought, 'After I am worn
out and my master is old, will I now have this
pleasure?'*

*Then the LORD said to Abraham, 'Why did Sarah
laugh and say, "Will I really have a child, now that
I am old?" Is anything too hard for the LORD? I
will return to you at the appointed time next year
and Sarah will have a son.'*

*Sarah was afraid, so she lied and said, 'I did not
laugh.'*

*But he said, 'Yes, you did laugh'* (Genesis 17:15 –
18:15).


Among Christians today there is a widespread
interest in miracles and a growing expectation to
see them happening. There is a new awareness of
the power of God over the whole of his creation
and a realization that we have too easily accepted
the world's restrictions on what can or cannot
happen. For too long scholars have played down
the supernatural ingredients of the Bible, or
relegated them to a past history with no relevance
to life today. 'Is anything too hard for the LORD?'
God challenges Sarai in 18:14, and we do well to
face that question head-on. It is a good check-up
on the vitality of our faith. Could God really give
Abraham and Sarai a child in their nineties? Quite
impossible, according to natural law; but God did
it (21:1–2).

There are dangers, though, in an oversuper-
ficiality here. Just as we had to note in the last
chapter that God was not appearing and speaking

audibly to Abraham every few days, that there were as many as thirteen years of silence, so we must realize that this miracle, great as it was, stood alone in Abraham's experience. Also, we must set it in its context, for it was the key event in the first stage of the fulfilment of the covenant promises, by which a nation would be created and the purposes of God, culminating in the coming of Christ, would be set in motion. The birth of Isaac was a vital ingredient in the chain of God's plan of salvation for mankind, so we are not dealing with a simple one-dimensional incident, such as an old woman miraculously conceiving a child. Much more is at stake than Sarai's personal joy. This is an important corrective to some contemporary notions of the miraculous, which seem to suggest that miracles are instantly available to those whose faith is great enough. It also corrects a wrong emphasis on our own personal joy and satisfaction, as though God were governing the universe on the principle of satisfying the whims and desires of his children. When we are told to 'name it and claim it', that physical health, material wealth and general well-being are the new-birth rights of the Christian if only we will exercise the faith to receive them, we are being invited to enter a world in which not only natural, but also spiritual, laws are suspended, in favour of our own personal comfort and happiness, by an indulgent God.

Of course God is not the prisoner of what we call 'natural laws', which are in fact only the observed uniformities of the created order. He decreed them in the first place. He is able to transcend or to overrule them, as he did in the birth of Isaac. But to imagine he would grant a child to couples of Abraham and Sarai's age as a regular response (provided they had sufficient faith) would be seriously to misunderstand God's providence. The normal restrictions to the age of child-bearing are built into our humanity as God created it, for the good of the mother, who needs to be reasonably young and robust both to give birth and to bring up the child, and also for the good of the child itself. To imagine that a 'given' of human life like that can be overturned by the desires of God's people, however holy or full of faith, is to imagine that the world is ruled by the wishes of Christians rather than the wisdom of God. That is a prospect which I, for one, find terrifying! I know Paul tells us in Romans 8:28 that 'in all things God works for the good of those who love him', but that is very different from saying God will give me whatever I want, if only I ask hard enough or work up sufficient 'faith' to earn it. It is God who works, by grace; not man, by subjective experiences of 'faith'. And God works for our good, not for our happiness or ease. Every parent knows the difference there. A dearly-loved child may be denied all sorts of things for his or her ultimate good, while a spoiled child may not be really loved at all. We live in a broken world, where suffering is the norm. We also live in a world where the grace of God is operative in wonderful ways and where his power is limitless. He can do 'immeasurably more than all we ask or imagine' (Ephesians 3:20), but he may not always choose to exercise that grace and power in the way we want. We have to live in that creative tension. Actually, it binds us closer and closer to God.

So when we face the question, 'Is anything too hard for the Lord?', and answer in faith, 'No', we are not shutting ourselves into a world where we affirm that God can draw a square circle. Faith is

106

not irrational, but supra-rational. It does not empty reality of its meaning, but penetrates to a deeper dimension. As it is part of God's loving providence to order his universe according to his own consistency of character, we should not judge his presence or involvement only in terms of the unusual or unexpected, and certainly not the capricious. The supernatural is experienced as much in the dependability of the natural world, with its normal processes, as it is in the occasional miraculous interventions of divine sovereignty. For there is something God cannot do. 'If we are faithless, he will remain faithful, for he cannot disown himself' (2 Timothy 2:13). He is utterly true to himself – to his character, to his Word with its promises and its warnings, and to his principles of dealing with men and women in his world.

## Why the delay?

To see this particular miracle in its biblical context, we need to ask why it happened at all. In his sovereign authority over his world, God could perfectly well have arranged for the child of promise to be born when Abraham and Sarai were at the normal age for parenthood. To have a father of 100 and a mother over ninety certainly marked Isaac out as an unusual, not to say unique, child. As he was the first member of the covenant family, it is wholly appropriate that his conception and birth should have been exceptional. But while that is clearly an ingredient in the long wait his parents had, it is not the only significance. Once again the New Testament helps us here. 'Against all hope, Abraham in hope believed and so became the father of many nations, just as it had been said to him' (Romans 4:18). Paul goes on to show us that Abraham was not living a super-pious existence, detached from the physical realities of life. He knew all that and faced it, in faith. Paul continues: 'Without weakening in his faith, he faced the fact that his body was as good as dead – since he was about a hundred years old – and that Sarah's womb was also dead. *Yet* he did not waver through unbelief regarding the promise of God, but was strengthened in his faith and gave glory to God, being fully persuaded that God had power to do what he had promised' (Romans 4:19–21). The lessons God was teaching Abraham and Sarai were for men and women of faith in every subsequent generation. The waiting time was a period which God gave them to strengthen their faith, and through their example, ours too. The birth of Isaac was far less of a problem to God than the development of faith in his servants.

This can help us to understand what we call delays in our own Christian experience. We pray to God, earnestly, believing that he will not deny us anything that is for our good. But sometimes it would not do us any good spiritually to have what God will eventually give us too soon. We need to be brought to the realization that nothing is too hard for the Lord, and he often gets us to that point by making us wait for him to act. My own church, which occupies a city-centre site in the main shopping street, was approached by property developers over a period of fifteen years, long before I arrived. They wanted to take over our site and rehouse us elsewhere. The congregation would have loved a new building, but not at the expense of this key location. So they hung on in faith as the old building decayed, believing God had called them to that site and that somehow he was able to provide a new building there, in spite of rocketing costs. Eventually, a redevelopment was proposed on that site, with a new church, including halls, rooms, *etc.*, over shops. Five years ago we moved into that marvellous provision of God, at a fraction of the cost of the whole development. During the planning and building (we were away from the site for over two years) there were many lessons of faith to learn, but God's timing in it all we can now see to have been perfect. Now the building is too small and we look at the cinema next door and wonder and wait. 'Is anything too hard for the Lord?' Of course not, but he knows the plans and he knows the timing. He has promised to build his church (Matthew 16:18). Our part is to trust and obey.

## Abraham's laughter

After giving to Abraham the covenant sign of circumcision, God confirms to him that the covenant son will be born to Sarai. She too is to have a change of name marking her change of status. Her new name is to be Sarah ('princess') because she will become, through Isaac's descendants, the mother of kings. Abraham's reaction is carefully recorded. He 'fell face down; he laughed and said to himself, "Will a son be born to a man a hundred years old? Will Sarah bear a child at the age of ninety?" ' (17:17). Was this really the faith Paul writes about in Romans 4? Does it not look more like unbelief?

The verb translated 'fell face down' is most commonly used in the Old Testament to express worship. To prostrate oneself before the Lord is the most appropriate posture for worship. Abraham's laughter, therefore, is to be read in terms of amazement and wonder at what God is going to do. The element of incredulity is not an absence of faith. Often in our lives what God chooses to do for us seems too good to be true, but it is not. The promise Abraham now receives more clearly than ever before is great, so great that he falls on his face in adoration before God. But it is also so paradoxical that he can only laugh. 'How fantastic that at this advanced age Sarah and I are going to see God fulfil his promises of grace in this amazing way!' There is a response of faith to God's promises which involves laughter and joy at the wonder of the fact that God should ever deal with people like us, and bless us so richly. That's faith.

However, it was still a faith lacking in strength. Abraham tries to steer God into something a little more reasonable. 'If only Ishmael might live under your blessing!' he suggests (verse 18). There were still many loose ends, unresolved questions mixed in with Abraham's developing faith. And God is never hard on our genuine struggles of this sort. He loves to fan a flickering faith into a strong flame. Taking up Abraham's anxiety he answers it directly but characteristically by saying 'Yes, but . . .' (verse 19a). How often God meets our anxieties and misunderstandings, our problems expressed in prayer, with 'Yes, but . . . '. 'Yes, so much is right, but Sarah will bear you a son and you will call him "he laughs" [Isaac]' (verse 19b). God has a better way than his servant can appreciate at present. Ishmael will be blessed as well, but Isaac is to be the covenant man. And then, having said the child will be born within the year, God terminates the interview. Abraham is told enough, but not everything. The promise is clearly given to encourage his faith; the details remain hidden. But his faith grows, as ours does, by submission of all his thinking and partial understanding to the sovereign will of God. And there is always one indispensable proof of the reality of that faith – obedience.

## Abraham's obedience

'On that very day Abraham took his son Ishmael and . . . every male in his household, and circumcised them, as God told him' (verse 23). There was no delay. As soon as God 'went up from him', Abraham carried out the Lord's instructions. Such instant obedience not only illustrates a lively, growing faith, but it also strengthens and reinforces it. So often the impact of God's Word is lost on us because we delay our obedience. We convince ourselves that we need a little longer to think things through, or a more convenient occasion to start carrying it out. We ought to take as our motto the instructions given by Mary the mother of Jesus to the servants at the wedding reception in Cana, where the wine had run out. 'Do whatever he [Jesus] tells you' (John 2:5). That is the only proper way for faith to express itself.

Through Abraham's obedience, God's covenant community was actually sealed and signed for the first time. It was a community of men from contrasting backgrounds. Some had accompanied him from Chaldea, some had been acquired in Egypt; some had been born in the land of promise. They were different ages – Abraham was ninety-nine and his son Ishmael was thirteen, for example. They were of different status – many were slaves and Abraham was their master. But they were all members of the covenant community on the same grounds, entering the same way, through faith and obedience. In this sense they pre-figure the multitude of Abraham's spiritual children who, over the past two millenia, have constituted the new covenant community, the church of Jesus Christ. The way in for all of us, whatever our race, age or status, is exactly the same: not through an outward rite of circumcision (though baptism marks our initiation into God's community) but through repentance and faith, issuing in submission and obedience to the lordship of Christ. All this is on the grounds of the grace of God through the cross of the Lord Jesus, just as it was God's grace that called and justified Abraham.

To us the challenge constantly comes to exercise our faith in obedience. Otherwise, like an unused muscle, it will atrophy. Disobedient Christians find their faith weakening, their doubts multiplying and their lives more full of difficulties than of certainties. But we do not have to give up our certainties to deal with our doubts. When we begin building on what we do know, by obedience, doing what God has already shown us, we shall find our faith strengthened to trust God for what we do not know, whether in the present or the unseen future.

## Sarah's laughter

It is midday. Abraham is resting in the entrance to his tent in the Grove of Mamre, where he and his extensive flocks are currently camped. Looking up, he unexpectedly sees three men. His reaction is very swift. He hurries out to meet them, bowing himself before them, offering them the courtesies and hospitality that might be extended to any traveller in the east – water to wash their feet and the provision of a meal. It may well be that Abraham recognized supernaturally that this was a visitation from Yahweh, for in addressing him he uses the title 'adonai' (my lord) which is frequently used of God in the Old Testament. Certainly the Scripture is clear later that one of the figures was the LORD (18:22), and that the other two 'men' were in fact angels (19:1). This would seem to be one of those rare pre-incarnation appearances of Christ which do sometimes occur in the Old Testament (*cf.* Joshua 5:13–15). But the hospitality that was offered was characteristic of bedouin generosity. When Hebrews 13:2 exhorts us, 'Do not forget to entertain strangers, for by so doing some people have entertained angels without knowing it', the writer's mind may well have gone back to this very incident. God loves to visit us in the everyday situations of life, not least because he knows all the details of just where we are and what we are doing.

As the three guests recline in the shade of the tree, Abraham bustles into the tent to start Sarah on baking some bread. Then he's out to the herd to select a 'choice, tender calf' for the menu. Some curds and milk complete the preparations of what is now a lavish meal, served personally by Abraham. It is rather more than the 'something to eat' of verse 5. Throughout their eating he stands, attentive, ready always to offer the most generous hospitality and the most personal service. We would want to do that if we knew that Jesus had come to eat with us. We would want to give him the very best, of course. But then he may well do so, as we 'entertain strangers'. For he told us that on the last day he will say to his faithful followers as they receive their inheritance, 'I was hungry and you gave me something to eat, I was thirsty and you gave me something to drink, I was a stranger and you invited me in' (Matthew 25:35).

The meal ends and the strangers ask where Sarah is. As any eastern lady would be, she is secluded behind the camel-hair curtain at the entrance to the tent, but well within earshot and doubtless agog at the mention of her name. 'Then the LORD said, "I will surely return to you about this time next year, and Sarah your wife will have a son" ' (verse 10a). That startles the eavesdropper, who laughs silently to herself at such an incredible suggestion. Sarah met the Lord's promise with sheer unbelief. She knew about God's promise to Abraham, but clearly she was not convinced by it; at least, she was not prepared to accept it for herself. Her attitude was one of cynicism: We are too old now to think about that happening. It seems as though her response was totally self-centred, without any deep interest in the nature of God's covenant purposes for Abraham and herself. This was not Abraham's laughter of amazement in faith, but the scornful laughter of resolute unbelief and, as such, it brought a stern rebuke from the Lord. 'Why did Sarah laugh? . . . Is anything too hard for the LORD?' (verses 13–14). Such unbelief in the face of God's promises amounts practically to atheism. To know that Yahweh is God and yet to laugh at what he promises is unbelief – it is to deny him. To imagine either that he cannot, or will not, keep his word is to slander his character and put ourselves under his judgment.

'Sarah was afraid, so she lied and said, "I did not laugh" ' (verse 15a). But that reaction, the fear that leads to a denial of her guilt, is answered in the most final way by the Lord. 'But he said, "Yes, you did laugh" ' (verse 15b). These are the only words recorded in the Bible that pass between God and Sarah. However, when we come to that great New Testament chapter of faith, Hebrews 11, we find that Sarah is definitely included. It was by faith that she was enabled to bear Isaac, though past age (Hebrews 11:11). I take this to indicate that the Lord's reproof brought her to her senses, and so to a personal faith that God would indeed fulfil his promise, even to and through her. God's reproofs are still his kindnesses towards our ignorance and unbelief, finding out the lack of faith and even cynicism which is so often deeply rooted in our minds and hearts, and shaming us into recognizing and eventually admitting what is wrong in order to bring us to trust him more completely.

It is significant too that God dealt with Sarah as an individual. Indeed, one of the main purposes of this special visitation was to deal with her unbelief. Abraham seems to have been so much more advanced in faith, but then he had received so many more spiritual privileges. It is not unusual within an engagement, or marriage, for one of the couple to be more advanced in the faith than the other. This was certainly the case here, but the fact that God specifically moved out to Sarah to include her in the covenant promise is surely an indication that his purpose is to develop and strengthen each individual's trust and so to build them together in faith. Marriage is one of God's creation ordinances and it is his plan that husband and wife should be united as one flesh, one unit for life, by their marriage, but also that they should be united in Christ so that whole families may come to faith. God was not content to leave Sarah lagging behind;

a husband or wife can therefore pray with certainty for the continuing growth to spiritual maturity of his or her partner.

## What about us?

'Is anything too hard for the LORD?' When we think of what his name means in terms of faithfulness and power, we know nothing is beyond him. There has not been one moment of time since the world first came into being when he has not governed and sustained it by his Word of power. There is not a promise he has ever failed to fulfil. We have not breathed a breath in our lifetime independently of God's will and grace. Nothing is impossible with God. So we must apply that truth to wherever we are in our own Christian experience.

We face many spiritual challenges. Perhaps it is the challenge of forgiveness. Can I ever be really clean from my sin? Can the past be buried? It may be the challenge of temptations that pull us down again and again – attitudes of mind we cannot change, habits we cannot alter. Coupled with this is the challenge to become more like Christ in our characters. We are so slow to learn that we despair of ourselves and wonder if Christ can ever change us. Or it could be a cloud of depression which seems never to lift. Will we ever see the light again? Perhaps it is an area of apparently unanswered prayer, where it seems useless to go on asking. 'Is anything too hard for the LORD?' Whatever the specifics of the challenge, that is what it comes down to in the end. That is the key question.

We have to say to ourselves, 'What has God said about it?' We have to look into the Bible to see what he has committed himself to do. If God says that those who believe in the Lord Jesus have eternal life and will not be condemned, but have passed from death to life (John 5:24), then God is committed to that and we must believe it. If the Bible declares that sin shall not be our master (Romans 6:14), then we can exercise faith and claim that deliverance. We do not need to become anxious about God's guidance for our future, because his Word gives us the clearest of patterns to follow. 'Trust in the Lord with all your heart and lean not on your own understanding; in all your ways acknowledge him, and he will make your paths straight' (Proverbs 3:5–6). If God has promised that he is able to make all grace abound to us so that we, having all that we need at every time, may abound to every good work (2 Corinthians 9:8), then we have to trust him to do that, whatever service he calls us to, whatever personal needs we may face. Find out what God says – that is faith's first task.

The second question is, 'Do we believe it?' If our laughter is in unbelief, then we exclude ourselves from all that God would give us. Not that our faith changes things; but God does, when we trust him. Sometimes there may not be any specific promises relating to that situation, but we must still trust God on the basis of all that we know about his character and all the promises he has given. All we can say then may be, 'Lord, your will be done; give me the grace you have promised to bear whatever burden you call me to carry.' That is the faith that proves the power of God, but it does not change his mind, or impose our will on his. How miserable we would be if it could! Which of us would ever dare to pray again? But if we trust where we cannot see and rely on God when we do not know the way, then he will work out his perfect will, and if that includes what would be called the impossible by men, it will happen (see Luke 18:27). Isaac, the son of laughter, will be born, but it will be the laughter of amazement and joy, not cynicism and unbelief. God can even change that! 'Is anything too hard for the LORD?'

# Chapter nine

# Prayer power

When the men got up to leave, they looked down toward Sodom, and Abraham walked along with them to see them on their way. Then the LORD said, 'Shall I hide from Abraham what I am about to do? Abraham will surely become a great and powerful nation, and all nations on earth will be blessed through him. For I have chosen him, so that he will direct his children and his household after him to keep the way of the LORD by doing what is right and just, so that the LORD will bring about for Abraham what he has promised him.'

Then the LORD said, 'The outcry against Sodom and Gomorrah is so great and their sin so grievous that I will go down and see if what they have done is as bad as the outcry that has reached me. If not, I will know.'

The men turned away and went towards Sodom, but Abraham remained standing before the LORD. Then Abraham approached him and said: 'Will you sweep away the righteous with the wicked? What if there are fifty righteous people in the city? Will you really sweep it away and not spare the place for the sake of the fifty righteous people in it? Far be it from you to do such a thing – to kill the righteous with the wicked, treating the righteous and the wicked alike. Far be it from you! Will not the Judge of all the earth do right?'

The LORD said, 'If I find fifty righteous people in the city of Sodom, I will spare the whole place for their sake.'

Then Abraham spoke up again: 'Now that I have been so bold as to speak to the LORD, though I am nothing but dust and ashes, what if the number of the righteous is five less than fifty? Will you destroy the whole city because of five people?'

'If I find forty-five there,' he said, 'I will not destroy it.'

Once again he spoke to him, 'What if only forty are found there?'

He said, 'For the sake of forty, I will not do it.'

Then he said, 'May the Lord not be angry, but let me speak. What if only thirty can be found there?'

He answered, 'I will not do it if I find thirty there.'

Abraham said, 'Now that I have been so bold as to speak to the Lord, what if only twenty can be found there?'

He said, 'For the sake of twenty, I will not destroy it.'

Then he said, 'May the LORD not be angry, but let me speak just once more. What if only ten can be found there?'

He answered, 'For the sake of ten, I will not destroy it.'

When the LORD had finished speaking with Abraham, he left, and Abraham returned home (Genesis 18:16–33).


My son was on his first school trip abroad, in the South of France. His group met some Arab traders who were selling trendy sunglasses at fifteen francs a time. Trying their hand at a spot of oriental bargaining, he and his friends beat the price down to ten francs. Agreed! The ten francs were handed over and duly pocketed, but the sunglasses were not. The price was too low. Only after the teacher's intervention, in a stream of highly fluent and highly coloured French prose, was the money retrieved, but the sunglasses remained.

The bargaining of the Arab markets is famous all over the world – a series of exchanges by which eventually a price is agreed. That is how some people have interpreted this incident. The dialogue with God on behalf of Sodom, which moves from fifty to forty-five to forty to thirty to twenty to ten in six exchanges, is seen as a fascinating example of eastern bargaining, showing in this primitive religious form (it is claimed) just how little man understood of the majesty or transcendence of God.

Whatever the structure may or may not owe to the cultural background, this is the first great example in the Bible of intercessory prayer, that is, prayer on behalf of other people. To see it as Abraham haggling with God is surely to misunderstand his motivation and God's purpose. For this event, as all the others, is recorded to illustrate the central theme of the Abraham story – the development of faith. It is not simply that when we pray God moves in the lives of other people to do things which otherwise would not have happened. Prayer is that – all of that – but it is not only that. Prayer also has an effect upon us. Prayer not only changes people and situations; it also changes the people who pray. Arguably the most important thing happening here is the expansion of Abraham's vision of God, so that when he leaves this prayer interview, which probably occupied a long period of time, he is not the same man. He is a man of increased faith.

## The roots of prayer

Prayer begins in our personal relationship with God. One of the most remarkable features of this prayer is that God took the initiative by revealing to Abraham the judgment which was about to fall on Sodom and Gomorrah. As Abraham conducted his guests along the way that led to the cities of the plain, the LORD not only revealed the perilous situation in which the cities were placed, but waited for Abraham's prayer, which he had himself initiated. God also terminated the discussion, deciding the point at which the matter would rest (verse 33).

Prayer is the means by which our personal relationship with God is fostered and developed. What is true of human relationships is equally true of man's relationship with God. The only way to get to know someone is by communication. It may be verbal or non-verbal, vocal or written, but there has to be both speaking and listening, a meeting of minds and hearts, for a relationship to grow. That is the pattern here. God speaks to Abraham, as he still does to us through his Word, by his Spirit. And our response is in prayer. Both ingredients are vital, but both are the product of God's grace. He moves us to pray and he enables us in our weakness and ignorance. 'We do not know what [or how] we ought to pray, but the Spirit himself intercedes for us with groans that words cannot express' (Romans 8:26). It is God who brings prayer concerns to our minds and God who waits for his people to intercede with him.

There is another insight into God's thoughts here, for we are told the motivation behind his decision to share with Abraham what he is about to do. It rests in the clause, 'For I have chosen him' (verse 19a). One of the ways by which Abraham will be a means of blessing to all the nations is by passing on God's revelation to future generations, and so God explains to his man what is about to happen as a further confirmation of his sovereign authority and power. The man whom God has chosen has a responsibility to 'direct his children and his household after him to keep the way of the LORD by doing what is right and just' (verse 19). The emphasis is upon God's friendship with Abraham – a relationship that had to be built every day and worked out in practical, dedicated and disciplined obedience. If we want to be people of prayer we have to be nurturing this foundational friendship with God all the time. And it takes time. Too often our prayers are little more than emergency 'phone calls to God, but there is a whole area of friendship with God, of being able to share our heart with God and learn his heart for us, which he longs for us to explore more and more.

As with Abraham, so with us, God wants to develop this personal relationship for the benefit of others. We are never the end of the line. He has other people he wants us to direct into his ways, for we each have unique circles of contact and influence. We should not see prayer as a duty, one of the ingredients of the Christian package which we have to accept. Rather, prayer is the means by which our living contact with God is deepened and enriched, and because we love him we want to know him better, to be more effective for him in the world, to count for God here and now. All that happens as we pray for other people.

## Justice and mercy

As the LORD shares with Abraham what is about to happen to Sodom, there is a lovely human touch in the vivid language that is used (verses 20–21). Accommodating himself to Abraham's finite limitations, God says he will visit Sodom to see if what they have done is as bad as the outcry that has reached him. Of course in his omniscience God already knew everything there was to know about Sodom, but the stress here is that judgment, which must inevitably fall on sin, is tempered with mercy. It is never hasty, but always perfectly informed so as to be utterly righteous. No individual can pull the wool over God's all-seeing eyes. No community can sin against God with a high hand and expect to get away with it, but his delay in judging is a mark of his mercy.

On the basis of this revelation of God's character, Abraham begins to intercede for the city. It is a reminder to us that we are never on stronger grounds in our intercessory prayer than when we appeal to God on the basis of his character, as revealed in his own Word. Abraham begins with a question. 'Will you sweep away the righteous with the wicked?' (verse 23). Behind it lies a deep personal concern for Lot, his nephew, who has been living in Sodom now for about twenty years. The New Testament tells us that Lot was 'a righteous man' and that he was 'distressed by the filthy lives of lawless men . . . tormented in his righteous soul by the lawless deeds he saw and heard' (2 Peter 2:7–8). So there is a concern for Lot, but behind that an even deeper concern for the glory of God's character. 'What if there are fifty righteous people in the city? Will you really sweep it away and not spare [or forgive] the place for the sake of the fifty righteous people in it? Far be it from you to do such a thing . . . treating the righteous and the wicked alike . . . Will not the Judge of all the earth do right?' (verses 24–25). The prayer is built entirely on the character of God, which is why it is so bold. What will the surrounding peoples make of the justice of Yahweh if all the inhabitants of Sodom are destroyed, irrespective of their personal behaviour?

Abraham has a passion for the glory of God. He wants to see his character vindicated and what is proposed does not seem to fit with that blend of justice and mercy which Abraham has come to know. So he pours out his difficulties and argues them honestly before the Lord.

Where did Abraham learn that sort of empathy and concern? Surely it was from the God who called him, the God who was constantly teaching him that he was the covenant man, not because of his worth but because of God's grace. It is as though Abraham is saying to God, 'Surely you cannot change your character now!' He has no problems with God's sovereign power – he is judge of all the earth. But surely the judge can be relied upon to act righteously, to dispense justice. How can the righteous then be destroyed along with the wicked? So often the question, 'Will not the Judge of all the earth do right?' (verse 25b) is quoted in order to show that even the most perplexing acts of God would be capable of being fully justified, if only we had the full picture. But that is not its context. It is a heartrending plea to God to be consistent with himself.

That is the sort of prayer God honours and answers. There is a right 'boldness', confidence or freedom of speech that God's children may and should use in coming to his throne of grace (Hebrews 4:16). We should never demand, never manipulate; but we can ask and we can plead, especially on the ground of God's self-revelation in Scripture. Although we may misunderstand his revelation, and our views may be spiritually immature, nevertheless we are to use it as the foundation of our prayers to the God of justice and mercy, and if we have got things wrong, 'that too God will make clear' to us (Philippians 3:15b).

## Persistent prayer

All true praying is persistent. Abraham's dialogue with God is marked by a blend of humility with boldness. Never for one moment does his confidence forget the realities of the relationship in which he is involved. 'I am nothing but dust and ashes' (verse 27); 'May the Lord not be angry, but let me speak' (verse 30); 'Now that I have been so bold as to speak to the Lord' (verse 31). The nearer we draw to God, the more we are humbled by his majesty. That is the position of power in prayer. If the angels veil themselves in God's presence, how much more do we need to abase ourselves in submission before him? Our very weakness and inability are among the strongest claims we have, and yet with them there is a shamelessness of faith, which appeals persistently to God and will not give up until the answer is clear. That is the sort of praying God loves. He did not withdraw. He heard

Abraham out and each time he answered positively, confirming his character.

Six times Abraham makes his request, but as the number of the righteous decreases from fifty to ten, so his faith is increasing as he edges his way forward with God. This is a great exploratory prayer, with Abraham pressing further and further into God's grace and mercy. At the same time, God is drawing Abraham on. As well as answering the prayer for Sodom, he is developing the faith of Abraham as he learns to trust the righteousness and mercy of the Lord. That is why this prayer is not a bargaining process. Abraham is not trying to influence God to do something he would otherwise not do. But that raises real problems for many of us about the validity and purpose of prayer. If God is going to act anyway, why pray?

Certainly it would not be true to say that if God's people do not pray God cannot work, because God is omnipotent. He does not need us; but he does graciously use us. So we know that our prayers do have an integral part to play in the outworking of God's purposes. It seems that God chooses to use his omnipotence to wait for his people to pray and that he chooses not to work, though of course he could, until his people seek his face, humble themselves before him and ask him to work on their own behalf and on the behalf of others (see 2 Chronicles 7:14). It is beyond question that where God's people pray like that, God works. Where they do not pray like that, they work – and the difference could hardly be greater.

Prayer does not change the mind of God, but it is his appointed means by which he involves us in his purposes, enabling us to share in their outworking, so that we have a part to play in situations being changed through our prayers. All this is because God has chosen to order his world in this way and has committed himself to answer the believing prayers of his people. We live in a world as ripe for God's judgment as ever Sodom was, but do we set ourselves to pray as Abraham did? If our praying is sporadic and we give up easily it can only be because our daily relationship with God is superficial and our understanding of his character is impoverished. If God finds our hearts so tepid and our will so fickle, perhaps what we call unanswered prayers, or delays, are really God's grace in stretching and developing this little faith we do have, by drawing us to pray more often and to trust him more. What is certain is that if we spent more time talking to the Lord about our families or friends, we would find that the time we spend talking to them about the Lord would be so much more fruitful and effective.

## But was it all worth it?

What did Abraham's prayer achieve? Chapter 19 of Genesis is the record of God's judgment falling on the cities of Sodom and Gomorrah in total destruction. The two angels who visit the city to investigate its state are met by righteous Lot sitting in the gateway, probably with the other elders. The alien seems to have risen to some prominence in Sodom, although his spirit was vexed by the immorality all around him. Not only does he offer hospitality to the visitors but he insists on it, knowing the dangers they would be subject to if they were to spend the night in the city square. But Lot's house is besieged by a mob demanding that the visitors should be handed over to them to have sex with them. His arguments are swept aside and Lot himself is only rescued by the two angels who strike the mob with blindness. Being warned that the LORD is about to destroy the city, Lot informs his sons-in-law who dismiss it as a joke. At dawn the angels virtually drag Lot, his wife and his two daughters from the city to find refuge in Zoar, while burning sulphur rains down on Sodom and Gomorrah from the LORD out of the heavens. The reluctance of the family to leave is symbolized by Lot's wife who lingered, looking back to Sodom, and who also seems to have been overwhelmed by the cataclysmic upheaval, perhaps as molten materials poured upon her, so that 'she became a pillar of salt'. The narrative ends with the picture of Abraham retracing his steps early the next morning to the place where he had interceded with the Lord. As he surveys the panorama before him the whole plain is enveloped in dense smoke, rising as from a furnace. But there is also one very significant comment. 'When God destroyed the cities of the plain, he remembered Abraham, and he brought Lot out of the catastrophe' (19:29).

Did God answer Abraham's prayer? Of course he did! Once again Abraham had been used to save Lot's life and the righteous man was rescued in spite of his unbelieving sons-in-law and his reluctant wife and daughters. Clearly these were the only righteous people God had found in the city and it seems that that was due more to family solidarity under Lot's headship than to a personal commitment to righteousness on their behalf. It was the mercy of God that prevented Lot from being infected by the evils of Sodom, which Ezekiel later described as 'arrogant, overfed and unconcerned; they did not help the poor and needy.

They . . . did detestable things before me' (Ezekiel 16:49–50). But Lot had made no impact for God on that pagan city. God had not placed him there – he had chosen for himself (13:11). That family would never have been rescued if the angels had not forced them out.

Abraham's prayer was answered. It should certainly encourage us to pray, for our situation is the same. 'It was the same in the days of Lot,' the Lord Jesus said. 'People were eating and drinking, buying and selling, planting and building. But the day Lot left Sodom, fire and sulphur rained down from heaven and destroyed them all. It will be just like this on the day the Son of Man is revealed' (Luke 17:28–30). God's judgment day is as certain a reality for our world as it was for Sodom and Gomorrah. Just as there is a heaven to be gained, so there is a hell to be shunned.

Our danger is that, like Lot, we become so infected by the scepticism of those around us, so bemused by the apparent security of life in Sodom, so attached to what we own, or to our status, that we hesitate to believe that judgment will ever come. Even when he did leave Sodom, Lot pleaded to be allowed to go to Zoar, rather than into the mountains as God had directed him. It was only a small town – it could not contain great wickedness – but it represented security to Lot. He was more secure living in a town with other people than launching out into the unknown with God. That alone shows what the years in Sodom had done to the faith of this righteous man. But he had an uncle who prayed for him. And when God's people pray, his angels are active everywhere. No-one is beyond his reach, if they will listen to his warnings. Who can tell what eternal rescues may yet be achieved in the lives of our families or friends if we learn to persist in intercessory prayer for them?

## Chapter ten

# Faith's failure—and victory

Now Abraham moved on from there into the region of the Negev and lived between Kadesh and Shur. For a while he stayed in Gerar, and there Abraham said of his wife Sarah, 'She is my sister.' Then Abimelech king of Gerar sent for Sarah and took her.

But God came to Abimelech in a dream one night and said to him, 'You are as good as dead because of the woman you have taken; she is a married woman.'

Now Abimelech had not gone near her, so he said, 'Lord, will you destroy an innocent nation? Did he not say to me, "She is my sister," and didn't she also say, "He is my brother"? I have done this with a clear conscience and clean hands.'

Then God said to him in the dream, 'Yes, I know you did this with a clear conscience, and so I have kept you from sinning against me. That is why I did not let you touch her. Now return the man's wife, for he is a prophet, and he will pray for you and you will live. But if you do not return her, you may be sure that you and all yours will die.'

Early the next morning Abimelech summoned all his officials, and when he told them all that had *happened, they were very much afraid. Then Abimelech called Abraham in and said, 'What have you done to us? How have I wronged you that you have brought such great guilt upon me and my kingdom? You have done things to me that should not be done.' And Abimelech asked Abraham, 'What was your reason for doing this?'*

*Abraham replied, 'I said to myself, "There is surely no fear of God in this place, and they will kill me because of my wife." Besides, she really is my sister, the daughter of my father though not of my mother; and she became my wife. And when God had me wander from my father's household, I said to her, "This is how you can show your love to me: Everywhere we go, say of me, 'He is my brother.' " '*

*Then Abimelech brought sheep and cattle and male and female slaves and gave them to Abraham, and he returned Sarah his wife to him. And Abimelech said, 'My land is before you; live wherever you like.'*

*To Sarah he said, 'I am giving your brother a thousand shekels of silver. This is to cover the offence against you before all who are with you; you are completely vindicated.'*

*Then Abraham prayed to God, and God healed Abimelech, his wife and his slave girls so they could have children again, for the LORD had closed up every womb in Abimelech's household because of Abraham's wife Sarah* (Genesis 20:1–18).

As we survey the life of Abraham we must never forget his crucial role in the unfolding drama that is the Old Testament. One way of looking at the thirty-nine books is to see them as God's continuous preparation of his people for the coming deliverer first promised in Genesis 3. With the fall of man into sin and the subsequent tyranny of the devil over humanity, the one ray of light among the curses which God pronounces is that the woman's offspring will crush the serpent's head. As God begins to prepare the way for the eventual victory of Christ in the cross and resurrection, he is resisted at every stage by the most devious satanic strategies. Nowhere is the devil more successful than in the human clay of God's people which he is able so often to distract and subvert from God's pathway in his forlorn attempts to prevent the divine promise from being fulfilled. Even the greatest men and women of God are not immune from his attacks. One has only to think of Moses' petulance, David's adultery, Elijah's depression and here, Abraham's faithlessness. It is so often at the point where we seem to be most strong that our weakness is most easily exposed. The man of faith is found to be faithless, and with the birth of the promised son only a matter of months away Abraham seems ready to risk losing everything in order to secure his own safety.

## Action replay?

We are not told why Abraham moved on from Mamre at this point. Perhaps the horror of the destruction of the cities of the plain so affected him that he could not stay there any longer. Perhaps he was forced to move to find fresh grazing for his flocks. But for whatever reason he travelled west, down from the hills towards the coastal plain and into the territory of the Philistines. There he camped in the foothills of the Judaean mountains near to Gerar, south-east of Gaza. Archaeological excavations have revealed a prosperous city of the Middle Bronze Age, the time of Abraham, about 18 km from Gaza. Here the local chief, Abimelech ('the king is my father'), took Sarah to be among his wives. The name 'Abimelech' is probably a cognomen of the Philistine kings, rather as 'Pharaoh' was of the Egyptian rulers. The situation is of course a replica of Abraham's earlier encounter in Egypt. But unlike that incident, nothing is said here about Sarah's beauty. Abimelech's motives seem to have been rather concerned with Abraham's wealth and the alliance he imagined he might contract with this prosperous nomadic chief, to his own advantage, by marrying his sister. Abraham had assured Abimelech that this was his relationship to Sarah. The situation is so similar that critics have suggested that the two accounts are 'doublets', that is, different tellings of the same story. They argue that nobody would make the same mistake twice. But that argument is weakened both by Derek Kidner's comment that 'it is easier to be consistent in theory than under fear of death', and by our own spiritual experience of how easily we fall repeatedly to the same temptations and weaknesses.

'But God came to Abimelech' (verse 3). The Lord intervenes to rescue Sarah, not because she or Abraham deserve it – she had been part of the conspiracy (verse 5) – but because not even the faithlessness of the covenant man will prevent the God of covenant reliability from fulfilling his promises to his people. In a dream, God threatens Abimelech's life because he has taken a married woman, albeit completely innocently. He may have been polygamous, but he was certainly not intending to be adulterous. It is this clear conscience of Abimelech which God has recognized, by keeping him from touching Sarah and now by warning him before he does. He must restore Sarah to Abraham immediately, or he and his dependants will die. There is a heavy irony in the contrast between the prayer that God will require Abraham to offer for Abimelech's deliverance and the open fellowship that characterized a different Abraham called to intercede for Sodom. Everything depends on our faithfulness to God and our practical trust in him.

At the first light of dawn Abimelech was up, explaining his dream to his terrified household and summoning Abraham to account for his actions. As always, the question 'why?' was foremost. Why have you brought us into such danger? Clearly Abraham had not thought beyond his own super-ficial self-centredness. The reason he had deceived Abimelech was to save his own skin. He was afraid that these pagans would kill him in order to take his wife, because 'there is surely no fear of God in this place'. Actually, he could not have been more wrong, as Abimelech's behaviour illustrates. The pagan king certainly feared God as he responded to the dream message. This reminds us that we are always wrong to judge from outward appearances, whether or not God will reveal himself to someone else. There is a God-shaped vacuum in the heart of every man and woman, created in God's image, to which he can communicate. But not only was Abraham's assessment of Abimelech quite wrong. More seriously, he had totally miscalculated what would happen if he chose to tell a lie rather than trust in God. He was relying on his own wisdom rather than doing what he knew was right, so that morally and spiritually he did not have a foot to stand on. The fact that he could have relied on God to keep his word and so preserve his life seems to have escaped him entirely. His only thought had been, 'How can I get myself out of this danger?'

Abraham's second reason is equally lame. On leaving Haran, Abraham and Sarah had made an arrangement that wherever they went they would assume the relationship of brother and sister. If it became known that Abraham was her husband, then his wife would become a target for any local chieftain who decided he wanted to add Sarah to his collection of wives. The fiction was based on the fact that Sarah was actually Abraham's half-sister, and although it was the product of cowardice it seemed to be the best way to guarantee Abraham's safety. After all, he argues, it was not untrue and a man must have some sort of security if his God makes him wander from his father's household (verse 13).

There is an Adam-like shift of the blame in that last interpretation of his life of faith. God had never made him wander aimlessly. There had always been a direction, always a purpose. Abimelech's response seems not to have been conditioned by the quality of Abraham's defence, which was negligible, so much as by his exaggerated respect for wealth and status. He gave lavishly to the man whose shame he had exposed because he did not want this man as his enemy. So as well as human slaves, sheep and cattle, Abimelech made a gift of a thousand silver shekels (about 11.5 kg), literally 'to cover' or 'to atone for' the offence. This is the verb (*kipper*) which later will be used throughout the Old Testament to express the action of atonement, by which sin is covered through the blood of the sacrifice. The wrong was recompensed, the guilt covered and Abraham was free to live wherever he chose in Abimelech's territory. 'Then Abraham prayed to God, and God healed Abimelech, his wife and his slave girls so they could have children again' (verse 17). By God's providence the situation is returned to what it was before Abraham's disastrous intervention, and the matter is closed.

## Talking tactics

Abraham's fall into temptation contains a number of warning notes which we would do well to heed. It came immediately in the wake of a special experience of God's presence and help. Who would have thought that after the depths of Abraham's communion with God as he interceded for Sodom, when he prayed and prayed and prayed, he could have fallen so quickly into faithlessness? But that is precisely what happened – and does happen to us. Just a few hours after the Last Supper, Simon Peter was denying with oaths that he had ever seen or known Jesus. The devil knows when to strike. He knows when we are spiritually prone to free-wheel, to relax, to imagine that because of some special mark of God's grace we don't need to watch and pray quite as much as we did. We rely on the experience of God we have had rather than exercising faith now, in a personal way, in God as we face new challenges.

It is also ironic, not to say poignant, that Sarah is put in danger by Abraham's ruse at the very point where the promise is about to be fulfilled. For these events happened during that important year between the angels' announcement and the actual birth of Isaac. Here is the covenant man endangering the promise itself just as it is about to come to its long-awaited fruition!

The devil also knows where to strike. So often his greatest successes are in the area of old unresolved conflicts, where past defeats or half victories come back to taunt us. It was probably nearly thirty years since Abraham had fallen into the same trap down in Egypt. During those thirty years, his relationship with God had developed tremendously. He had become the friend of God, a man of great faith. But whoever we are and whatever our spiritual privileges, we must never forget that in this world we are always open to temptation. However long we have experienced victory over sin, the moment we move outside of God's will or cease to abide in Christ and trust his grace, we are immediately prone to every sort of danger. Every Christian has areas of weakness in which a moment's compromise can mean playing with fire. Temptation often stirs up old conflicts. That pact Abraham had agreed with Sarah should have been cancelled long ago. It was a pact of faithlessness. Surely over the years he had learned that he did not need that, that they did not need to be living a lie when their lives were in the hands of the living God who would defend and keep them? But it seems as though that part of their lives was never really dealt with, and so it returned to plague Abraham again. We need to know our weaknesses, to remember where we have fallen in the past and to be ruthless and radical in dealing with those areas of past defeat. We need to run to Christ for his strengthening power and victorious grace whenever we face testings in those areas, or the devil will come back and use them over and over again to make us fall. In such situations, the most dangerous thing to do is to rationalize and so excuse our compromise. 'Besides, she really is my sister. . .' (verse 12). Abraham spoke those words in order to convey a false impression, and that is the essence of lying.

However, the most important dimension of the whole incident is the attack on the character of God which lay at its heart. God's promises and Sarah's safety both paled into insignificance alongside Abraham's selfishness. He decided to follow his own wisdom rather than to trust in God, and that course of action is always dishonouring to God. The disasters that overtake us are often of our own making, because we have chosen to walk by sight rather than by faith. Doubtless Abraham's faith was well known among the pagan tribes, and certainly Abimelech knew who this God was who appeared to him in his dream. He knew who Abraham's Lord was, but what was he to think of Yahweh if his servant's standards were actually lower than those of the pagan king himself? One of the chief ways in which the devil still attacks the honour and glory of our God is by the moral inconsistencies and sin tolerated in the lives of those who profess to be his servants. None of us is strong enough to stand for a moment apart from the grace of God through the Holy Spirit in our lives. That is why we need to lean hard on God's resources every day of our lives.

However, let us also never forget that this God goes on bothering with friends of his who let him down. The Holy Spirit is showing us through Scripture that giants of faith like Abraham (and that is what he was, in comparison with us) were nevertheless ordinary people. It was in spite of Abraham's natural self that he became the friend of God, not because of it. So when we look at ourselves as very raw material for sainthood and wonder why on earth God should go on bothering with us, we are only being realistic. We are the most unpromising stuff. What this God loves to do, though, is to demonstrate his creative power and sheer ingenuity by taking people who let him down and who deserve nothing of his grace, to show what he can do with the most resistant life that is prepared to let God be God. He does not need our assistance. He does not call for it. He has no favourites. What he does for others, he will do for each of us. If he can make a man like Abraham his friend, with all his weaknesses, then he can remake us into the image of Jesus Christ, sons and daughters who reflect the family likeness. All he asks us to do is to trust him and so obey him. Then we can get back onto the main line, for the real action of the story.

\* \* \*

*Now the LORD was gracious to Sarah as he had said, and the LORD did for Sarah what he had promised. Sarah became pregnant and bore a son to Abraham in his old age, at the very time God had promised him. Abraham gave the name Isaac to the son Sarah bore him. When his son Isaac was eight days old, Abraham circumcised him, as God commanded him. Abraham was a hundred years old when his son Isaac was born to him.*

*Sarah said, 'God has brought me laughter, and everyone who hears about this will laugh with me.' And she added, 'Who would have said to Abraham that Sarah would nurse children? Yet I have borne him a son in his old age.'*

*The child grew and was weaned, and on the day*

Isaac was weaned Abraham held a great feast. But Sarah saw that the son whom Hagar the Eygptian had borne to Abraham was mocking, and she said to Abraham, 'Get rid of that slave woman and her son, for that slave woman's son will never share in the inheritance with my son Isaac.'

The matter distressed Abraham greatly because it concerned his son. But God said to him, 'Do not be so distressed about the boy and your maidservant. Listen to whatever Sarah tells you, because it is through Isaac that your offspring will be reckoned. I will make the son of the maidservant into a nation also, because he is your offspring.'

Early the next morning Abraham took some food and a skin of water and gave them to Hagar. He set them on her shoulders and then sent her off with the boy. She went on her way and wandered in the desert of Beersheba.

When the water in the skin was gone, she put the boy under one of the bushes. Then she went off and sat down nearby, about a bow-shot away, for she thought, 'I cannot watch the boy die.' And as she sat there nearby, she began to sob.

God heard the boy crying, and the angel of God called to Hagar from heaven and said to her, 'What is the matter, Hagar? Do not be afraid; God has heard the boy crying as he lies there. Lift the boy up and take him by the hand, for I will make him into a great nation.'

Then God opened her eyes and she saw a well of water. So she went and filled the skin with water and gave the boy a drink.

God was with the boy as he grew up. He lived in the desert and became an archer. While he was living in the Desert of Paran, his mother got a wife for him from Egypt (Genesis 21:1–21).

The real action always lies with God. He is the master scriptwriter, the only director who can fit all the ingredients of life together into a coherent whole. Abraham's story, like ours, features the God who is always coming in with his grace and mercy. He sets the pace. He determines the content. He sees to it that through all the changing scenes of life what matters most, that personal relationship with himself which is eternal life (John 17:3), is constantly being developed. And so Abraham is constantly being exhorted, encouraged and enabled to have faith in God.

## Solid rock

At last the long-promised, long-awaited event occurred. Ever since we first met Abraham this has loomed large on the horizon. 'I will make you', God said, 'into a great nation.' We have seen the false starts, the inadequate faith, the incredulity which this promise has provoked over the years, but now at last God vindicates his word. Three times it is stressed that this birth is the fulfilment of the divine promise. 'The LORD was gracious to Sarah *as he had said*, and the LORD did for Sarah *what he had promised* . . . at the very time *God had promised*' (verses 1–2, italics mine). We are not left in any doubt as to why this amazing event happened. Therefore, we are not to live our lives in any doubt that what God promises he performs. Our faith is both stimulated by the Word of God and finds its anchor in his unchanging truth. We are in danger of forgetting that in many Christian circles today, which explains why our faith is so anaemic and why we have to rely on visible evidences of God's presence and power, with the resultant danger that we walk by sight, not faith at all.

There is a great famine of the Word of God today around the world. The irony is that in an age which has the Bible available in more languages than ever before, when biblical research is more developed than ever before, when there are more Christian books and teaching aids, and when communication has developed a sophistication undreamed of just a few years ago, many Christians probably know their Bibles less well and read them less than for many generations. The habit of daily Bible reading has never been established by many of Christ's followers. In many churches, preaching has been downgraded in favour of more active participation in worship, so that it is becoming increasingly rare to find evangelical churches where the Bible is taken seriously enough for a period of time to be set aside in the worship service to 'read, mark, learn and inwardly digest' its teaching. Of course, there has been much dull and indifferent preaching and sadly there still is. But the answer to that is better preaching, more biblical preaching, more relevant and applied preaching, not less. Congregations need to be fed on the Word of God. If we think we can do without the Bible we shall be spiritual pygmies, for there is no nutritional substitute. We cannot know God's Word too well or trust it too much. We cannot build more securely than on God's self-revelation in Scripture, for what Scripture says, God says, and the least of his whispers in Scripture is solid rock on which to ground our lives.

But we can only be sure of God's Word when we are often in the Scriptures. 'What does the Bible say?' should be the first question to spring to the

Christian's mind about any issue, because therein is to be found the mind of God. As we pray that the Holy Spirit, who inspired the authors of Scripture, will open our minds as we read to understand God's message, there can be a meeting between ourselves and the Lord every time we open our Bibles. That is how faith grows and spiritual maturity develops. The alternative is to rely on other people or on ourselves, and that ultimately means impoverishment. Of course God can speak to us through other people, but how are we to judge when another Christian comes to us and says, 'I really feel you ought to take this action', or even, 'The Lord has told me to tell you to do X'? If we do not have the objectively given revelation of God in his Word by which to judge, we are thrown back on someone else's ideas which may be right or wrong but are certainly not infallible. Or we are thrown back on our own subjective feelings, which are notoriously fickle. So often Christians look at circumstances that have come together and think it strange that this should happen and that should happen and deduce, 'It must be God saying something to me.' It may well be, but it is not necessarily so. The advice of friends and circumstantial evidences both need to be tested by Scripture. Not by searching desperately for a proof text, which is often out of context and so becomes a pretext, but by the whole weight of God's revelation and specific passages pointing to God's answers as we seek his will in prayer. The only solid rock on which we can rely absolutely is what God has promised in his Word, understood in its true context and interpreted by the guidance of the Holy Spirit. If God has said it, we can rely on it. Other Christians can be wrong. Circumstances may point in conflicting directions. Our emotional experiences in prayer may be confirming our desires rather than God's will. But God's Word alone is an infallible light to our path which will never lead us astray.

## A time to laugh

The birth of Isaac is also all about God's grace. The delay that Abraham and Sarah experienced, we must remember, was not to make them good enough, or worthy, to receive the fulfilment of the promise. Isaac was a gift of God's grace. However strong our faith may grow, it will never be the ground on which God works in our lives, though it may be the key. Grace precedes faith. That is true of our personal salvation. Saving faith in Jesus, which God grants as a free gift, is itself an evidence of his grace. So when Isaac was born, it was at God's set time. There was in fact no delay from God's perspective. He knew the time the child would be born when he first made the promise thirty years earlier, and now was the strategic moment. None of those years had been wasted. None had been unnecessary in the purposes which God was fulfilling in Abraham's life. So faith is not something we do in order to persuade God to act. It is simply taking God at his word and letting him work out the time scheme. What we call waiting, he calls trusting.

As God gave the child, so he had already named him (17:19). Isaac ('he laughs') spoke about the child's birth and existence. The laughter sprang from the incongruity of the child being born to this elderly couple and yet the joy of its reality. On the one hand there was the physical inability of Sarah and Abraham and on the other the bare word of

God's promise. But the birth of the boy, a miracle of grace and a demonstration of God's power, would make all who heard of it laugh with joy at the grace and power of a God who can do such things, who makes and keeps promises. So too for Sarah the name which might have rebuked her for her unbelief becomes a source of joy. 'God has brought me laughter' (21:6a), she exclaims. We must never forget that where God's grace exists, there is joy. Whenever a newborn Christian is added to the family of faith, if there is 'rejoicing in the presence of the angels of God' (Luke 15:10), surely there should be joy and laughter in the church on earth. It is a travesty of Christianity to imagine that holiness is measured by length of face! Thank God for all the joy that he pours into our lives. It should be a mark of us as Christians that we have an increasing capacity for rejoicing, for fun and laughter, for our God 'richly provides us with everything for our enjoyment' (1 Timothy 6:17).

## A time to weep

Our joys in this world are real, but they are mingled with sorrows. If they were not, we might become chained to this world rather than seeing beyond it. 'The child grew and was weaned, and . . . Abraham held a great feast. But Sarah saw that the son whom Hagar the Eygptian had borne to Abraham was mocking . . .' (21:8–9). The problem is not hard to imagine. Isaac, the toddler, the centre of attention, is the darling of the camp. Ishmael, the teenager, about sixteen now, the son of a slave, is severely displaced. No longer has he any hope of being Abraham's heir. This little boy has come and taken over his place and his aspirations. The verb 'he was mocking' is an intensive form of the verb from which Isaac's name comes. Ishmael mocked the very idea of this little child being the father of a great nation. This was the laughter of cynical unbelief, mixed with blatant jealousy.

Sarah, who had endured Ishmael's presence with his mother all these years, seized the opportunity with both hands. She insisted that Abraham should 'get rid of that slave woman and her son, for [he] will never share in the inheritance with my son Isaac' (verse 10). And Abraham was caught on the horns of a dilemma. That slave woman's son was his son too. He had all the natural ties of affection for Ishmael. Had he not asked God that Ishmael might live under his blessing, and had God not promised to bless and prosper the boy? It was no wonder that Abraham was greatly distressed by the problem. But, as he so often does at a time of great emotional need, God came to meet Abraham in his problem. The Lord reminded his servant of the promises he had already received. That was how God answered the problem. He guided Abraham to solve the problem of what he did not know on the basis of what he did know. And what he did know was what God had already said and done. There was the promise that 'through Isaac . . . your offspring will be reckoned' (verse 12), but there was also the promise to make Ishmael a nation too (verse 13). Ishmael would be blessed, but the covenant line would run through Isaac alone.

God reminds Abraham that this is the working out of what he has been shown already, so he has to trust God with the outcome and not be guided by his emotions or his partial understanding. It is the familiar pattern. God is working on and on in

Abraham's life, in situation after situation, until all the human props are removed and only God remains. He demonstrates his faithfulness by reminding Abraham of the promise and applying it to the problem in hand. Sarah had seen the reality of the situation, although her spirit of bitter retaliation was very far removed from God's. There was only one way. So early the next day Hagar and Ishmael are ejected from the camp with food and water to wander in the desert of Beersheba.

There is, however, another dimension to this which is expounded by Paul in Galatians 4. In that context, centuries later, he was facing Jews who considered it impossible that Gentiles should be admitted to God's covenant community, becoming his children and heirs of the promises. Gentile Christians were fiercely attacked and persecuted by the Jews, and even some Hebrew Christians wanted to make them submit to circumcision and other requirements of the ceremonial law before they would accept them as members of the church. Before long, Jerusalem would be destroyed by the Roman legions in AD 70 and the Jewish nation would be scattered. The old covenant with its tangible and visible expressions of the law would be removed, cast aside by God. To make his point Paul develops by analogy the story of Hagar and Sarah, using them to symbolize the two covenants. 'Now Hagar stands for Mount Sinai in Arabia and corresponds to the present city of Jerusalem, because she is in slavery with her children' (Galatians 4:25). She is representative of what Judaism had become – a religion of legalism, a slavery in which God's merit could only be earned by law-keeping. That had never been God's intention, but by centuries of distortion the old covenant had been made into a bondage. However, Sarah, the free woman, represents the new covenant of God's free grace in the good news of the Lord Jesus Christ. The one is a covenant of law leading to slavery; the other a covenant of grace leading to freedom. Paul's point is that the two cannot co-exist. When Isaac arrived, Ishmael had to go. That was God's way.

The New Testament application is that when Christ came and completed his work on the cross and through the empty tomb, bearing our sins and rising again to make us right with God, any thought of trying to win our way to God by being good enough or trying to deserve God's blessing had to go. Works cannot co-exist with faith as a means of being made right with God. There can be no marriage of the two. (Of course, in New Testament terms that is only half the story. Whilst it is true that works are never the means of justification, they are always its evidence and fruit. In that sense works must co-exist with faith, if faith is genuine. This is the argument of James 2:14–26, where Abraham's works are quoted as evidence of the genuineness of the faith by which he was accounted righteous. But while we must always bear that balance in mind, it is not the thrust of the argument in Galatians.) So Paul's conclusion is to ask, 'What does the Scripture say? "Get rid of the slave woman and her son, for the slave woman's son will never share in the inheritance with the free woman's son." Therefore, brothers, we are not children of the slave woman, but of the free woman. It is for freedom that Christ has set us free. Stand firm, then, and do not let yourselves be burdened again by a yoke of slavery' (Galatians 4:30–5:1).

The significance for us is still considerable.

Ishmael had to leave the camp because he was not the child of the promise. The child of grace alone, not the offspring of human works, could inherit the covenant promises. That is why God told Abraham to expel Hagar and Ishmael. Therefore, if we want to be among God's covenant people, it can only be by faith in the promises of God. We are Christians only because of our response of faith to the grace of God, not by works of righteousness which we have done. That is the only way into the Christian life, and it is the only way on. So many of us as Christians lose our joy, our laughter, our freedom, because although we know we are saved by grace alone, through faith, we are always attempting to secure God's blessing by what we do. We are still trying to be good enough for God. But the Christian life does not depend on the rules of the particular Christian sub-culture we happen to find ourselves in, or on observing the traditions of men. That is not the way to live the Christian life. If we trust in the Lord Jesus, we have a full salvation in him. We are free to be our new, true, redeemed selves in Christ. We are not working towards sonship, hoping that one day we may be good enough for God. He has already made us his heirs, adopting us into his family, and we work out our salvation from that position. Isaac's right was his by birth. So with the Christian, the assurance of being accepted by God depends upon our new birth, on all that we are because through faith we are in Christ. This is the freedom which we must never give up for a yoke of slavery. We are to get rid of the slave woman since Christ has set us free. We are to give up our shares in the old Adam Improvement Society, which is a bankrupt concern, and allow Christ, who alone can meet our impossible debts, to put us in the right with God. As Paul expressed it elsewhere, 'It is we [Christians] who are the circumcision, we who worship by the Spirit of God, who glory in Christ Jesus, and who put no confidence in the flesh' (Philippians 3:3).

## Care for the outcast

The end of the story provides a moving picture of God's compassion. Although in covenant terms Ishmael was rejected, he was not ignored. As F. W. Faber put it, 'the love of God is broader than the measures of man's mind'. No sooner had Hagar and Ishmael been evicted than God began to bless them. They had quickly come to the end of their meagre resources, but not to the end of Yahweh's care. The sight of Ishmael dying of thirst and his mother sobbing in despair, unable to watch him die, moved the heart of God, as all human need undoubtedly does. But there was more to it than inarticulate need. 'God heard the boy crying' (21:17a) – not weeping uncontrollably like his mother, but calling out to God to have mercy. As that cry of extreme need was heard, an angel was sent to Hagar – not to the boy, but to the mother who was in the greater distress – in order to bring to her the loving kindness and faithfulness of Abraham's God. God heard Ishmael and in answer to his cry he opened Hagar's eyes and she saw a well (verse 19a). The immediate need was met, and on a long-term basis, for hers was a well at which life could be sustained. But there is a third statement of God's intervention which is more wonderful still. 'God was with the boy as he grew up' (verse 20a). Each divine initiative provides a step out of want and despair into the experience of God's personal provision and presence, a lifestyle undergirded by the unconditional promise, 'I will make him into a great nation' (verse 18b). That's grace.

It was also God keeping his promise to Abraham. There were lessons to be learned in the departure of Hagar and Ishmael, but they were not sent out into the unknown, bereft of care and resources. In the place of an empty water-skin God provides a well. Instead of certain death God provides a future. Ishmael lived in the desert and became a skilled archer. And in time Hagar found him a wife – in Egypt, where else? Finally, instead of living under Sarah's jealous scrutiny, Ishmael grew up in God's presence. When God calls us to obey, we can trust him with the consequences, however unpredictable or indeed impossible they may seem to us at the time. Marvellous things happen when we respond to God's grace in faith and obedience, for our God always keeps his promises. You can rely upon his word. That was what Abraham needed to know more clearly than ever before as he faced the greatest test of all.

## Chapter eleven

# The ultimate test

*Some time later God tested Abraham. He said to him, 'Abraham!' 'Here I am,' he replied.*

*Then God said, 'Take your son, your only son Isaac, whom you love, and go to the region of Moriah. Sacrifice him there as a burnt offering on one of the mountains I will tell you about.'*

*Early the next morning Abraham got up and saddled his donkey. He took with him two of his servants and his son Isaac. When he had cut enough wood for the burnt offering, he set out for the place God had told him about. On the third day Abraham looked up and saw the place in the distance. He said to his servants, 'Stay here with the donkey while I and the boy go over there. We will worship and then we will come back to you.'*

*Abraham took the wood for the burnt offering and placed it on his son Isaac, and he himself carried the fire and the knife. As the two of them went on together, Isaac spoke up and said to his father Abraham, 'Father?'*

*'Yes, my son?' Abraham replied.*

*'The fire and wood are here,' Isaac said, 'but where is the lamb for the burnt offering?'*

*Abraham answered, 'God himself will provide the*

*lamb for the burnt offering, my son.' And the two of them went on together.*

*When they reached the place God had told him about, Abraham built an altar there and arranged the wood on it. He bound his son Isaac and laid him on the altar, on top of the wood. Then he reached out his hand and took the knife to slay his son. But the angel of the LORD called out to him from heaven, 'Abraham! Abraham!'*

*'Here I am,' he replied.*

*'Do not lay a hand on the boy,' he said. 'Do not do anything to him. Now I know that you fear God, because you have not withheld from me your son, your only son.'*

*Abraham looked up and there in a thicket he saw a ram caught by its horns. He went over and took the ram and sacrificed it as a burnt offering instead of his son. So Abraham called that place 'The LORD will provide'. And to this day it is said, 'On the mountain of the LORD it will be provided.'*

*The angel of the LORD called to Abraham from heaven a second time and said, 'I swear by myself, declares the LORD, that because you have done this and have not withheld your son, your only son, I will surely bless you and make your descendants as numerous as the stars in the sky and as the sand on the seashore. Your descendants will take possession of the cities of their enemies, and through your offspring all nations on earth will be blessed, because you have obeyed me'* (Genesis 22:1–18).

'Faith is being sure of what we hope for and certain of what we do not see' (Hebrews 11:1). The greatest of all the unseen realities is the person and character of God himself. Therefore faith is at its most fully developed when it is prepared to trust God in the face of all the 'seen' evidence, to put his will first whatever the heart or the head may be saying. This is the ultimate test, presented by this extraordinary incident, which was to bring Abraham to the mountain-top in his long climb of faith with his Lord. It is inexplicable apart from the fact that the man who believed God was responding to a direct summons from his commander. *God* said, 'Take your son . . . Sacrifice him . . . ' (verse 2). These are the key words we must keep before us if we are to make spiritual sense of this story. Faith obeys God, whatever he may demand. That is not to say that faith is reckless or irrational. We would certainly distort the whole passage if we imagined this to be some extravagant gesture on Abraham's part to prove the reality of his faith in Yahweh. This was not an idea formed in Abraham's consciousness. It was not an imitation of the human sacrifices practised by the Canaanite tribes by which Abraham would prove his equal or greater devotion to his God. Nor was it a temptation that originated from the devil. The word came from God, the personal God of covenant faithfulness, with whom Abraham had been walking in fellowship for decades. That was why he had to fulfil it. It came as a test (verse 1) to prove the quality of his trust.

We need to grasp the divine origin of Abraham's conviction, not only to make spiritual sense of the story, but also to guard us from misleading applications to our own lives. There is a certain sort of 'spirituality' which imagines that the more outlandish, or even eccentric, a course of action appears to be, the more likely it is to be spiritually right. For example, Christians have given up jobs and homes because 'God told them' to do so and then have waited, sometimes for years, to be shown what the next step should be. Such a course of action has the attraction of looking very spiritual – launching out in faith, holding on to nothing. It can appeal to our pride and status in the Christian community. The crucial question to ask is, 'How do I know *God* has told me to do this?' My own judgment is highly fallible. I know how easily I can delude myself into thinking that what I want to do is, in fact, God's will. And if I am persuaded and persuasive enough, there will always be plenty of others to agree with me and reinforce my thinking. What I must not do is to move out into some life-changing decision without being as sure as I can reasonably expect to be that God has called me to take that step. He may call me to make some quite extraordinary sacrifices, but their extraordinary quality does not necessarily mean that they are of God. They may come from my own subconscious desires to imitate others whom I admire, or even to draw attention to myself, to win kudos among my friends.

We need to be careful as well as faithful in the stewardship of life's resources which God has entrusted to us, because it can take years to recover lost ground when a wrong turn is taken, often in headstrong defiance of wiser advice, from what are basically selfish motives. The degree of sacrifice involved is probably the best test of whether or not this is God's will. When a young man with no ties tells me that he is being called to work abroad as a missionary and that his 'guidance' is his boredom and lack of achievement in his present job, he needs to be made to think again. That may be God's call or it may be his daydream. How much sacrifice is being demanded?

For Abraham, the challenges involved were overwhelming. For thirty years he had waited for the birth of Isaac. By any human standards this boy was especially precious to his elderly parents, but added to their natural affection was all the content of God's covenant promises and commitment to him. At God's command, Abraham had removed his other son, Ishmael, from the camp, so that everything now centred on Isaac. All the promises God had made about Abraham being the father of a great nation and possessing the land depended on Isaac's continuance. And now the same God was demanding the incredible – the sacrifice of this son, his only son, his much-loved son (verse 2). Surely the heart of the test is there. The disincentives to obey God were not only that Isaac meant everything to his father, nor that the old man's pilgrimage would be reduced to meaningless rubble if Isaac were killed, but that God was apparently acting in a way contrary to everything Abraham thought he knew about him. That must have been the hardest test of all. In the past, God had usually prepared Abraham for some new step of obedience by revealing something more of himself or reminding him of promises already given; but not this time. There is just a clear, unmistakable summons to the father of a multitude to sacrifice his only son on a faraway mountain peak. What was God doing? Our image must not be of a puppeteer playing with Abraham, pulling the strings. Rather, we should think of a sports coach extracting the maximum effort from his champion athlete and then just that little bit more, over and above, to make him invincible.

## Faith in action

The immediate and deliberate obedience exercised by Abraham is very impressive. There was no delay, no arguing. All that was needed for the journey from Beersheba to Jerusalem, about twenty hours' walking, was prepared, even to the wood for the burnt offering. On the third day the little party of four saw the land of Moriah in the distance. This was the name given to the mountainous country round about what was to be the city of Jerusalem. On this mountain Solomon would later build his temple on the site of the threshing-floor where God had appeared to his father David (2 Chronicles 3:1). From this city, at a still later date, a much-loved only son would go out carrying the wood on which his life would be sacrificed for the sins of the whole world.

If Abraham's journey demanded faith every step of the way, his instructions to his servants provide a marvellous insight into his thinking at that time. 'I and the boy . . . will worship and then we will come back to you' (verse 5). This was no bluff, pretending that all would be well. It was a robust assertion of faith, grounded in the conviction that God would be faithful to his word. Abraham knew that what he was doing was an act of worship and he knew the God he was worshipping. What he was doing was in obedience to God's command and therefore to God's glory, and he was prepared to trust God with the consequences. That did not mean, however, that he had closed his mind to what might happen or that his was a blind faith in which mental processes had no place. The writer to the Hebrews in the New Testament helps us here. 'Abraham reasoned that God could raise the dead, and figuratively speaking, he did receive Isaac back from death' (Hebrews 11:19). Abraham was trusting God to fulfil his promises. The logic was really very simple, but what faith it required to follow it through! God had promised that his offspring would be reckoned through Isaac (21:12). Therefore, if Isaac was sacrificed, God must be going to raise him from the dead. Abraham knew that God would keep his promise. He had the circumstances wrong, but the theology was absolutely right.

So father and son separate themselves from the servants and press on together to the appointed place of sacrifice. The wood is carried by Isaac, but the instruments of sacrifice (the fire and the knife) are carried by Abraham. And Isaac asks his poignant question, 'The fire and wood are here, but where is the lamb?' (verse 7). The Holy Spirit does not mean us to miss one detail of what this obedience was costing Abraham. Surely his heart must have been breaking under the load, but he answers with magnificent faith, 'God himself will provide the lamb, my son' (verse 8). This is the faith we have watched growing, as small as a grain of mustard seed to start with, but exercised, stretched and developed now to maturity. 'God will provide' – that is faith!

This reply also supplies us with a spiritual principle which we all need to build into our own walk with God. Every Christian faces situations in which God's commands seem to contradict his promises, when all we have been building on up to that time seems threatened and about to collapse. What are we to do when we face that sort of crisis? The answer from Abraham is that we both believe the promise *and* obey the command. Trust and obey is the principle. That is always the response God calls for. We do not have to work out the circumstances in detail. Those can be left with God. Our part is to trust what God has said and on that foundation to press forward in obedience, knowing that 'God will provide . . . '.

So the top of the mountain is reached, the altar is built, the wood is arranged, and as the last act of preparation Isaac is bound and laid on the altar. 'Then he reached out his hand and took the knife to slay his son' (verse 10). The narrative is almost a succession of 'stills' as we are taken step by step to its climax. That was the response God had looked for – a full-hearted trust that took every step in conscious dependence on him. And as God was not disappointed in what he found in Abraham, neither was Abraham disappointed in his Lord.

## The Lord who provides

The drama is intense. At the very last moment, as Abraham stands poised with the knife over the covenant son, bound like a lamb on the altar, God breaks in. The angel of the LORD calls to Abraham from heaven to stop and to do his son no harm. 'Now I know that you fear God, because you have not withheld from me your son, your only son' (verse 12b). That has been the heart of the matter and now the test has been passed and the issue is beyond dispute. The man of faith has proved, as he could in no other way, that he will reverence God and obey his commands, even when he cannot understand what God is doing with him.

It is faith like that which proves the faithfulness of God. The sacrifice of Isaac had already been accomplished in Abraham's heart and he had met

God's requirements fully. Once that was settled, Abraham's eyes were directed towards the lamb, caught by its horns in a bush, which he had dared to expect God to provide. The offering that made the sacrifice was thus provided by God, not by Abraham, as a substitute for his son, Isaac.

If Abraham had been prepared to go to the last detail in obedience to God, then not one detail of his own provision had been overlooked by the Lord. The meaning of the incident is summed up by Abraham's naming of the place 'Jehovah-jireh', meaning 'Yahweh sees', or as it is more usually translated, 'the LORD provides'. The idea is that the LORD who sees the need will also see to it that the need is met by his own divine provision. 'And to this day it is said, "On the mountain of the LORD it will be provided" ' (verse 14b).

For us, as New Testament Christians, the whole incident is rich with an even deeper dimension of meaning. For on that very mountain where the temple later stood and where, year by year, countless animal sacrifices were offered to God to cover the sins of his erring people, what mankind most needed was provided by the God who 'sees to it'. The only reason that sacrifice was required in worship at all was because of human sin. Abraham and Isaac were both sinners who had inherited a fallen human nature from Adam. They could only draw near to a holy God, whose very righteousness would consume them, when the blood of sacrifice had been shed and a substitute had died in their place. Although the meaning and purpose of the sacrificial system is not explained until the time of Moses, later in the Pentateuch, God was still dealing with his covenant family on covenant principles even at this early stage. In a judicial sense

Isaac deserved to die, as a sinner, though his death could have had no sacrificial merit for anyone else and it could not even have atoned for his own sin. It would simply have represented the just punishment of sin, under which sentence every human being comes. But God provided a lamb 'instead of' Isaac. As we put ourselves in Isaac's position, as it were, under the knife and deserving to be cut off from God eternally because of our sins (the spiritual death of which physical death is the sign or sympton), we too are in a desperate condition, from which only a substitute can save us.

So we travel down the centuries from Abraham to the same location, around the year AD 33. A young man, an only son, a dearly loved son, is leaving the bustling city of Jerusalem to die as an atoning sacrifice, not roped to an altar but nailed to a Roman cross. The only begotten Son of God, Jesus Christ, is the lamb provided by God, not to deal with one man's sin, or a family's, or even a nation's, but to take away the sin of the world (John 1:29). He has lived a life of moral and spiritual perfection. He has always fulfilled the Father's will, so that he is unique among men in having no sins of his own for which to die. He can bring what no animal sacrifice could ever provide, however spotless and without blemish its body might be, that is, a perfect will to offer in the place of our rebellious human wills. There is no lamb provided for Jesus. He is himself God's provision, dying as our substitute, in our place, so that we might know God's forgiveness on a basis of righteousness, our sin atoned for and our guilt purged. If we can imagine a little of the agonies Abraham went through as an earthly father called upon to be willing to sacrifice his son, what must it have cost

God the Father to send the Lord Jesus to be the atoning sacrifice for our sins?

The Lord has seen to it; he *has* provided. The penalty of separation from a just and holy God, which our sins rightly deserve, has been fully met by Jesus in his death on the cross. Because he was forsaken, we may be forgiven. God has provided the substitute and, in Christ, he has achieved all that was necessary for rebels like us to be reconciled to God and brought into the intimacy of sons and daughters, within the family circle. The new covenant community is open to all who put their faith in Jesus as God's provision for sinners, and who obey him as their Lord and Master. The message is the same for us as it was for Abraham. Believe God's promises, trust yourself to him and obey his commands.

## Promises renewed

With the sacrifice of the ram completed, the angel of the LORD addressed Abraham a second time, to renew his former promises and to confirm them by an oath. It would be easy to see these blessings as a reward for Abraham's faith ('because you have done this . . . I will surely bless you', verses 16–17). But the promises were made long ago, when God first called Abraham to be the covenant man (12:1–3), and all the story in between has been of their progressive fulfilment. The promises are always the expression of God's grace, never the reward for Abraham's faith. But the other side of that coin is that the promises can only be enjoyed and experienced when they are met by faith and obedience.

The same principle still holds true for us. All the

promises of God are always potentially available for all of his people. As Paul puts it, 'No matter how many promises God has made, they are "Yes" in Christ. And so through him the "Amen" is spoken by us to the glory of God' (2 Corinthians 1:20). The birthright of the members of the new covenant is that the Father's resources are unrestrictedly theirs, provided they are appropriated by faith and in obedience. We live in the enjoyment of covenant blessings only as we exercise faith in God and obey his commandments.

Part of the renewed blessing for Abraham here is the way in which God chooses to underline its unchangeability, in the phrase, 'I swear by myself' (verse 16a). This is a unique occasion in the record of God's dealings with the patriarchs and as such is often referred to in the subsequent history (e.g. 24:7; 26:3; 50:24). It is further confirmed by the fact that this is a solemn declaration of the LORD, and as the promises are intensified in this way, so they are expanded in substance. To the promise that Abraham's descendants will be as numerous as the stars in the sky is added, 'and as the sand on the seashore'. They are also promised great victories over their enemies and the possession of their cities, as they conquer and occupy the land that God has promised. For Abraham the divine oath, grounded in the character of the God whom he has learned to trust more and more, must have been the greatest source of renewed comfort and strength.

The ultimate test had been passed with flying colours. But it was not an arbitrary event in Abraham's experience. It was vital to his continuing life of faith and important to his position in the unfolding history of salvation. In receiving Isaac back 'from the dead', Abraham learned more deeply that the much-loved son was a gift of God's grace. His life was in God's hands, not Abraham's, and as with every good gift of God there had to be a readiness at any time to give back to God what he had lent. And if Isaac is the son of the covenant, there are lessons for us, children of the new covenant by God's grace, in terms of our own surrender to the will of God. Those who would live in the enjoyment of covenant blessings must be prepared to place everything, even their own lives, on the altar of sacrifice. Our confidence can be in the same God, who still provides. 'He who did not spare his own Son, but gave him up for us all – how will he not also, along with him, graciously give us all things?' (Romans 8:32).

# Chapter twelve

# Finding God's guidance

*Abraham was now old and well advanced in years, and the LORD had blessed him in every way. He said to the chief servant in his household, the one in charge of all that he had, 'Put your hand under my thigh. I want you to swear by the LORD, the God of heaven and the God of earth, that you will not get a wife for my son from the daughters of the Canaanites, among whom I am living, but will go to my country and my own relatives and get a wife for my son Isaac.'*

*The servant asked him, 'What if the woman is unwilling to come back with me to this land? Shall I then take your son back to the country you came from?'*

*'Make sure that you do not take my son back there,' Abraham said. 'The LORD, the God of heaven, who brought me out of my father's household and my native land and who spoke to me and promised me on oath, saying, "To your offspring I will give this land" – he will send his angel before you so that you can get a wife for my son from there. If the woman is unwilling to come back with you, then you will be released from this oath of mine. Only do not take my son back there.' So the*

*servant put his hand under the thigh of his master
Abraham and swore an oath to him concerning this
matter.*

*Then the servant took ten of his master's camels
and left, taking with him all kinds of good things
from his master. He set out for Aram Naharaim and
made his way to the town of Nahor. He made the
camels kneel down near the well outside the town;
it was towards evening, the time the women go out
to draw water* (Genesis 24:1–11).

Abraham never forgot his origins. Perhaps it was
because of his semi-nomadic existence, perhaps
because of his growing awareness that God's
purposes through him were to be much wider in
these kin of his than he had at first imagined. Some
time after God's confirmation of his promises, news
reached Abraham about his brother Nahor, whose
wife, Milcah, had borne him eight sons (22:20–23).
Whether this set his mind thinking about the future
of his own son or not, we don't know. The death
of Sarah intervened (Genesis 23), and by the time
Isaac reached marriageable age Abraham was 'well
advanced in years'.

Humanly speaking, it was unlikely at that time
of life that Abraham would be launching out on
new initiatives. His old age and wealth could well
have provided a recipe for quietly sitting out his
remaining years, looking back in gratitude. But
Abraham was a man of faith. He was always
looking forward, pressing on by every means at his
disposal in the direction of the fulfilment of God's
promises. So for us, if faith has been growing at
every stage of our Christian experience, we need
not fear that the process will stop when we reach

old age. Abraham became increasingly conscious that the next stage of the promise had to be fulfilled, and for that to happen Isaac must have a wife. But whom could he select? Clearly none of Abraham's slaves was suitable, and it was out of the question for the son of the covenant to marry a Canaanite woman. The man of faith does not sit back and wait passively. Abraham was never a man to do that. Instead he begins to fulfil his responsibility, to act on the basis of what God has already revealed.

## Identifying the initiative

He decides to find a wife for Isaac from among his brother's family back in Chaldea. The chief servant (possibly Eliezer, see 15:2) is summoned and made to swear a solemn oath, by the LORD, that Isaac will marry a wife only from among Abraham's family. In addition she must come to him; he is not to return to that land. This was important not only for the continuance of the covenant line, but for the establishment of the covenant family as a distinct unit, living by faith in the land of promise. From this time onwards the prohibition of intermarriage with those who are not within the covenant community, who are not Yahweh's people, becomes a biblical principle. 'Do not intermarry with them. Do not give your daughters to their sons or take their daughters for your sons, for they will turn your sons away from following me to serve other gods' (Deuteronomy 7:3–4). The same rule governs marriage for the Christian. A Christian woman 'is free to marry anyone she wishes, but he must belong to the Lord' (1 Corinthians 7:39b).

Doubtless Abraham was aware that he was acting in accordance with what God had already revealed of his will, and that is always a prime requirement if we are to experience God's guidance in our detailed decision-making. Abraham cannot see what the outcome will be of the chain of events he is setting in motion, but he has learned enough in the school of faith to know that if he acts on God's promises and obeys his commands, he can trust God with the outcome. So he assures his servant, '[God] will send his angel before you so that you can get a wife for my son' (verse 7b). Because God will not go back on his word, Abraham must not go back on his commitment. If this door does not open then a better one will and the servant will be released from his oath. But on no account must the promise be doubted or the commands disobeyed ('Do not take my son back there', verse 8b). So the oath is sworn, the camel train assembled and the long journey back to the town of Nahor in Paddan Aram (north-west Mesopotamia) begins.

Faith has placed the responsibility for the outcome with God, where it truly belongs. The earthly servant equally has his part to play, diligently and conscientiously, but always in the knowledge that God will provide a wife for Isaac just as years before he provided a lamb. All true faith illustrates that blend of activity and trust. We have to work to our maximum capacity and ability, as though everything depended on us, but at the same time we rest in faith, knowing that ultimately everything depends on God. That is why all our forward movements, especially in the big decisions of life, like choosing a marriage partner, need to be prayed about, worked through on the principles of Scripture and constantly committed to God. Then we

170

can relax, knowing that all the details hidden from us are being planned by the Lord, who knows us and our situation far better than we ourselves could ever do. In that relationship we shall be prepared to go forward, one step at a time, with God.

\*      \*      \*

*Then he prayed, 'O Lord, God of my master Abraham, give me success today, and show kindness to my master Abraham. See, I am standing beside this spring, and the daughters of the townspeople are coming out to draw water. May it be that when I say to a girl, "Please let down your jar that I may have a drink," and she says, "Drink, and I'll water your camels too" – let her be the one you have chosen for your servant Isaac. By this I will know that you have shown kindness to my master.'*

*Before he had finished praying, Rebekah came out with her jar on her shoulder. She was the daughter of Bethuel son of Milcah, who was the wife of Abraham's brother Nahor. The girl was very beautiful, a virgin; no man had ever lain with her. She went down to the spring, filled her jar and came up again.*

*The servant hurried to meet her and said, 'Please give me a little water from your jar.'*

*'Drink, my lord,' she said, and quickly lowered the jar to her hands and gave him a drink.*

*After she had given him a drink, she said, 'I'll draw water for your camels too, until they have finished drinking.' So she quickly emptied her jar into the trough, ran back to the well to draw more water, and drew enough for all his camels. Without saying a word, the man watched her closely to learn whether or not the* LORD *had made his journey successful* (Genesis 24:12–21).

## Clarifying the guidance

Having arrived at the township, the servant immediately proves himself to be Abraham's servant in more than name by consulting Abraham's God. It is his relationship with Abraham which has brought him into the covenant community and marked him with the covenant-sign of circumcision (17:13). On these grounds he approaches Yahweh to ask for success and a clear sign of his guidance.

The sign in itself was not spectacular, but it would have been unusual enough to be quite unmistakable. In other words, the servant was not asking for a supernatural manifestation of God's will. He was not looking for flashing lights or neon signs, or expecting to hear inner voices – all of which would be notoriously unreliable anyway. What he asked for was an ordinary human action which would reveal a most unusual quality of character. The chosen bride for Isaac was not only to give the stranger a drink when he requested it, but to offer to water his camels too. The first part of the request might be expected in the normal run of hospitality, but it would be an unusually generous-hearted girl who would offer voluntarily to draw enough water to satisfy ten thirsty camels. She would make an ideal wife for Isaac – or anyone!

The sign requested, then, was an indication of character, not a supernatural intervention, which would enable the servant to make the right choice in accordance with the will of God, and so for the blessing of Isaac. Again, we are to learn the normality of the walk of faith. Our contemporary tendency to value guidance according to how dramatic, unusual, even irrational or crazy it appears, may owe something to our culture, but it owes very little to Scripture. God most often guides through what might be called mere common sense, but which is actually the application of the mind God has given us to the patterns of the ordered world of cause and effect which he has created and sustains.

'Before he had finished praying, Rebekah came out . . .' (verse 15a). Sometimes it's like that! Abraham had to wait thirty years for Isaac, but the servant does not have to wait at all for Isaac's wife. Perhaps this was a special mark of God's grace to someone who was beginning to exercise a personal faith, but who was not nearly as far down that road as his master, Abraham. Often in our early days of Christian experience our prayers seem to be answered with greater rapidity than later on. But the fact of the matter is that God is in control, and what accords with his will determines when and how the answers come. Faith learns to leave the timing with God.

Rebekah was the daughter of Bethuel, himself the son of Nahor and therefore Abraham's nephew. As the servant hurried towards this beautiful girl with his request for a drink, he must have been amazed to hear the script flow word-perfect from her lips, just as he had requested. Whether he was stunned by the answer, or just sensibly cautious, he was certainly not bowled over by what had happened. He 'watched her closely to learn whether or not the LORD had made his journey successful' (verse 21).

He provides a very helpful example for us all.

Although the sign he asked for was so quickly granted, he did not give himself up blindly to first impressions. He still used his judgment and discretion, tested the circumstances and weighed the whole situation carefully. That was not lack of faith so much as an expression of the depth of his commitment to the will of God alone. He knew how important his task was, and how critical it was for him to keep in touch with God all the way through the process. While we have no right to ask God for signs merely to gratify our curiosity, we can ask him to indicate his will for us with great clarity through our everyday circumstances, but not by arbitrary, out-of-the-blue events. God does not bypass the mind. The servant's guidance was a spiritual interpretation of an ordinary human event. That is one reason why we have the Bible. It is not a magic book out of which phrases suddenly jump to become our guidance. The Bible provides us with the principles by which we think through life's decisions, on our knees, with God. So, when God gives us a green light it is usually made up of a mixture of the message of Scripture, the advice of other respected Christians, the opening of doors of opportunity, all coming together by the Spirit to give us an increasing inner conviction which is tested and proved over a period of time. The spectacular in guidance is not necessarily stronger. It may actually be more vulnerable since it can be more subjective. We can all too easily convince ourselves that what we want must correspond to God's will for us.

\*     \*     \*

*When the camels had finished drinking, the man*

took out a gold nose ring weighing a beka and two gold bracelets weighing ten shekels. Then he asked, 'Whose daughter are you? Please tell me, is there room in your father's house for us to spend the night?'

She answered him, 'I am the daughter of Bethuel, the son that Milcah bore to Nahor.' And she added, 'We have plenty of straw and fodder, as well as room for you to spend the night.'

Then the man bowed down and worshipped the LORD, saying, 'Praise be to the LORD, the God of my master Abraham, who has not abandoned his kindness and faithfulness to my master. As for me, the LORD has led me on the journey to the house of my master's relatives.'

The girl ran and told her mother's household about these things. Now Rebekah had a brother named Laban, and he hurried out to the man at the spring. As soon as he had seen the nose ring, and the bracelets on his sister's arms, and had heard Rebekah tell what the man said to her, he went out to the man and found him standing by the camels near the spring. 'Come, you who are blessed by the LORD,' he said. 'Why are you standing out here? I have prepared the house and a place for the camels' (Genesis 24:22–31).

## Confirming the course

As the servant rewarded Rebekah's kindness with some incredibly generous gifts, he discovered not only that she was representative of a family that was more than willing to offer hospitality, but also that God had led him to the daughter of Abraham's nephew, so fulfilling in detail his master's concern that Isaac's wife should be found from among his own people. His response was to worship God. There was not an ounce of self-congratulation, only an amazed gratitude to God who had shown kindness not only to his master but to him personally. 'As for me, the LORD has led me . . . ' (verse 27). The adventure of faith into which his master had pressed him had brought him personal answers to his prayers which began to build his own faith, as he saw further irrefutable evidences of God's character. Now it was not just Abraham's God but his God too whom he knew to be faithful to his word and steadfast in his loving care. As he looked back he could see that every step was part of the master plan. There was never a cul-de-sac, nor a blind alley. So although it may be a long and arduous journey before we see why and how God's plans are working out, not one step is wasted when we walk with him.

Rebekah ran back home to tell the astonished family her good news, and one sight of the golden ring and bracelets was enough to bring brother Laban out to the well. The welcome could hardly have been more cordial. Had he noticed the heavily-laden camels too? Later encounters with Laban in Genesis 29–31 indicate that he was never slow off the blocks when there was something in it for himself. But he was certainly right in describing the servant as 'blessed by the LORD' (verse 31a), for there can be few greater privileges than knowing God's guidance in our lives. Yet that is the real possibility set before every covenant child of God. In whatever area of life – marriage, career, family, housing, Christian service, retirement – God is willing to lead us every step, if we will let him. The secret is to walk with him today so that he can put us wherever he wants us tomorrow, at the right time, in the right place. He promises to guide on the journey if the governing principle of all our travelling is 'by faith'.

* * *

*So the man went to the house, and the camels were unloaded. Straw and fodder were brought for the camels, and water for him and his men to wash their feet. Then food was set before him, but he said, 'I will not eat until I have told you what I have to say.'*

*'Then tell us,' Laban said.*

*So he said, 'I am Abraham's servant. The L*ORD *has blessed my master abundantly, and he has become wealthy. He has given him sheep and cattle, silver and gold, menservants and maidservants, and camels and donkeys. My master's wife Sarah has borne him a son in her old age, and he has given him everything he owns. And my master made me swear on oath, and said, "You must not get a wife for my son from the daughters of the Canaanites, in whose land I live, but go to my father's family and to my own clan, and get a wife for my son."*

*'Then I asked my master, "What if the woman will not come back with me?"*

*'He replied, "The L*ORD, *before whom I have walked, will send his angel with you and make your journey a success, so that you can get a wife for my son from my own clan and from my father's family. Then, when you go to my clan, you will be released from my oath even if they refuse to give her to you – you will be released from my oath."*

*'When I came to the spring today, I said, "O* LORD, *God of my master Abraham, if you will, please grant success to the journey on which I have come. See, I am standing beside this spring; if a*

*maiden comes out to draw water and I say to her, 'Please let me drink a little water from your jar,' and if she says to me, 'Drink, and I'll draw water for your camels too,' let her be the one the Lord has chosen for my master's son."*

*'Before I finished praying in my heart, Rebekah came out, with her jar on her shoulder. She went down to the spring and <u>drew water</u>, and I said to her, "Please give me a drink."*

*'She quickly lowered her jar from her shoulder and said, "Drink, and I'll water your camels too." So I drank, and she watered the camels also.*

*'I asked her, "Whose daughter are you?"*

*'She said, "The daughter of Bethuel son of Nahor, whom Milcah bore to him."*

*'Then I put the ring on her nose and the bracelets on her arms, and I bowed down and worshipped the Lord. I praised the Lord, the God of my master Abraham, who had led me on the right road to get the granddaughter of my master's brother for his son. Now if you will show kindness and faithfulness to my master, tell me; and if not, tell me, so I may know which way to turn'* (Genesis 24:32–49).

## Presenting the evidence

The focus of the narrative now shifts onto Rebekah and her family. How are they to be equally sure that it really is God's purpose for her to leave her home and travel with the servant to meet an unknown bridegroom in a strange and foreign land? The answer is contained in the evidence which Abraham's servant presents to them. It is worth commenting on how detailed that was and how transparently honest and sincere was his presentation. He let the story speak for itself, without trying either to flatter or cajole. Yet there was an urgency about his manner which made him share his story before he was willing to eat. The fact that he put his mission before his own comfort must have lent even greater conviction to what he said. But God did not expect Rebekah's family to respond without hearing and analysing the evidence. He is not in the business of coercion.

First, the servant introduced himself in relationship to their relative and his master, Abraham; but the whole story he went on to tell centred on the LORD and all that he had done. He spoke of Abraham's great wealth, but attributed it all to God's abundant blessing. The presents which Rebekah had received were not just an impressive, 'one-off' display. They indicated a man of great resources on whom God's blessing was resting. Rebekah would be joining a wealthy family, but more importantly, a godly family, too. Abraham's faith had not declined since he left his family; it had only grown and flourished. The evidence of this was the special circumstances surrounding Isaac's birth, the child of Sarah's old age and Abraham's sole heir. From this his hearers could infer how Yahweh's special blessing and promise rested on Abraham and on his family. A child born against the normal course of nature was divinely appointed to fulfil God's ongoing purposes, in which Rebekah too might now become involved.

Then the servant recounted how he had been led to them. The solemn oath sworn to Abraham was remembered, with its emphasis upon the special choice of his own family. They had not been chosen by accident. Nor were they at the end of a long list of interviewees. Rebekah was the first and only choice, in answer to the combined prayer of master

179

and servant that the LORD would bring this mission to a successful conclusion. The servant's prayer had been answered immediately and in specific detail. Rebekah had fully demonstrated the sort of character for which he had been praying and when she revealed her identity, the servant had been brought to his knees in worship. He no longer had any doubts. As far as he was concerned all the evidences pointed to the fact that Rebekah was Yahweh's choice of a wife for Isaac, but still he put himself and his mission in his hearers' hands. ' "Now if you will show kindness and faithfulness to my master, tell me; and if not, tell me, so I may know which way to turn" ' (verse 49).

As we put all these factors together, we can build up a pattern to help us in our understanding of what God's guidance may be, as it is presented to us by someone else. Today it is not uncommon for Christians to be presented with a 'word from the Lord' by other Christians, but how can such claims be assessed? We should look for a transparent honesty and sincerity in their approach. Where there is spiritual reality there is neither need nor room for man-made pressures, emotional arm-twisting or spiritual manipulation. There should also be a willingness to let the hearer come to a free decision as the evidence is weighed, trusting that if the guidance is really of God there will be a unanimity of mind and spirit. Then there should be valid testimony about the Lord's involvement in the situation, how he has already guided and provided and above all what tangible answers to prayer there have been. Finally, the situation or proposed course of action should be susceptible to rational and spiritual understanding, showing it to be something that can be undertaken honourably and sensibly, under God's continued guidance and help.

These safeguards are not the product of unbelief but of a faith that really wants to honour God. All too often faith is caricatured as gullibility – trying to believe something that is just not true. But if you suddenly drive into a bank of fog on a motorway and the warning lights advise you to drop your speed to 20 mph, it is not an act of faith to drive on at 60 mph, firmly persuaded that God will look after you. That would be an act of folly. We need to be wise in our assessment of every situation, especially when guidance about the future is the issue.

\*     \*     \*

*Laban and Bethuel answered, 'This is from the LORD; we can say nothing to you one way or the other. Here is Rebekah; take her and go, and let her become the wife of your master's son, as the LORD has directed.'*

*When Abraham's servant heard what they said, he bowed down to the ground before the LORD. Then the servant brought out gold and silver jewellery and articles of clothing and gave them to Rebekah; he also gave costly gifts to her brother and to her mother. Then he and the men who were with him ate and drank and spent the night there.*

*When they got up the next morning, he said, 'Send me on my way to my master.'*

*But her brother and her mother replied, 'Let the girl remain with us ten days or so; then you may go.'*

*But he said to them, 'Do not detain me, now that the LORD has granted success to my journey. Send me on my way so I may go to my master.'*

*Then they said, 'Let's call the girl and ask her about it.' So they called Rebekah and asked her, 'Will you go with this man?'*

*'I will go,' she said.*

*So they sent their sister Rebekah on her way, along with her nurse and Abraham's servant and his men. And they blessed Rebekah and said to her,*

> *'Our sister, may you increase*
> *to thousands upon thousands;*
> *may your offspring possess*
> *the gates of their enemies.'*

*Then Rebekah and her maids got ready and mounted their camels and went back with the man. So the servant took Rebekah and left* (Genesis 24:50–61).

## Taking the decision

As Laban and Bethuel, his father, listened to the servant's story, they were left in no doubt. 'This is from the LORD' (verse 50a). Each of the parties, being sensitive to God's direction, confirmed and corroborated the other's guidance. Again this is something we should expect to happen in a situation where both are concerned to understand what God's will is. Within a church or any Christian group, a large measure of unanimity about major decisions is something we should both expect and prize highly, provided the body as a whole is prayerfully asking for God's guidance and ready to do whatever he reveals. There is, after all, little point in praying for his direction if we have reservations about what we will or will not accept. The impressive quality about the response from Rebekah's family was that they knew that when God indicated his will it had to be carried out, although their personal faith was nothing like as fully developed as Abraham's. Their reply could hardly have been more open and direct. 'Here is Rebekah; take her and go, and let her become the wife of your master's son, as the LORD has directed' (verse 51). So, when we are sure of what God is saying, there is nothing to be gained from any obedience that is not both prompt and total. Too often we are found praying for guidance when the way is clear. What we really need is to trust and obey. For example, we do not need to ask God whether or not we should be involved in the work of evangelism. The great commission still stands and the needs of unreached peoples all around the world are immense. Our prayers should be for strength to obey and wisdom to channel our individual contribution where God wants it to be.

Abraham's servant, overwhelmed by this successful conclusion to his expedition so soon, was again brought to prostrate himself before the LORD in gratitude. It is a reminder of the importance of thankfulness, which is so often overlooked. We are all good at earnest prayer when we are in a desperate situation, facing difficulties, or needing urgently to know God's guidance. But like the ten lepers healed by Jesus (Luke 17:11–19), the vast majority of us do not return to give thanks to God when those prayers are answered. And yet to worship the Lord from a grateful heart for all his kindness and goodness, to pour out our praise and love to him, is more acceptable to God than all our sacrifices.

Having slept on their decision, however, Laban had second thoughts next morning and with Rebekah's mother, significantly included at this point, he asked for a ten-day delay before the party left. At one level this is very understandable. It would seem that the mother had not been consulted the night before. She would obviously feel most deeply the loss of Rebekah from the family home, and at such short notice, too. There would be few mothers who would not identify with her need of time to come to terms with what was happening.

However, the servant saw danger in the delay. It would be harder to leave after ten days and the problem might then arise as to whether Rebekah would go at all. If the Lord's guidance had been so clear then there was no doubt as to what his will was. What advantage would there be in making it harder to fulfil that will by delaying? In the end the choice was left with Rebekah herself, who seems to have been consulted for the first time about her own future at this point in the narrative.

Interestingly enough, contemporary marriage contracts from the period indicate that the bride's commitment was required before the marriage could be ratified. 'I will go' was Rebekah's response, and to their great credit the family no longer stood in her way. Nor did they grudge her going. They gave her a great send-off along with her nurse, Deborah, who was to remain in the family and eventually died in the household of Rebekah's son, Jacob (35:8), and her maids. As the procession left the city the blessings of Rebekah's family rang in her ears, reiterating the covenant promises of Yahweh to Abraham in which Rebekah was so soon to be involved. 'May you increase to thousands upon thousands; may your offspring possess the gates of their enemies' (verse 60).

It is a great thing in life to acknowledge and

follow God's will joyfully and cheerfully. Though we are not always promised the prosperity and security which Rebekah's family wished on her in material terms, yet those who follow God's plans for their lives, at whatever personal or material cost, are certain to experience the fulfilment and well-being (*shalom*) which is the spiritual blessing of God, both in this world and beyond.

\* \* \*

*Now Isaac had come from Beer Lahai Roi, for he was living in the Negev. He went out to the field one evening to meditate, and as he looked up, he saw camels approaching. Rebekah also looked up and saw Isaac. She got down from her camel and asked the servant, 'Who is that man in the field coming to meet us?'*

*'He is my master,' the servant answered. So she took her veil and covered herself.*

*Then the servant told Isaac all he had done. Isaac brought her into the tent of his mother Sarah, and he married Rebekah. So she became his wife, and he loved her; and Isaac was comforted after his mother's death* (Genesis 24:62–67).

## Welcoming the bride

The last act of this marvellously vivid drama is as colourful and visual as all that has preceded it. Isaac, out in the field at sunset, thinking and praying, looked up and saw the camel-train on the horizon. Before they met Rebekah veiled herself as a mark of modesty and dismounted from her camel as a mark of respect, in order to meet and greet her future husband. We can imagine the eagerness with which the servant related to Isaac the extraordinary circumstances of Rebekah's discovery and the many evidences of God's guidance.

Because God does not make mistakes, we need have no doubt that Isaac and Rebekah were not disappointed in one another. But just as it had been Rebekah's choice to come, so it was Isaac's to receive and to marry her. He was not coerced. He chose to pledge himself to her as his wife and he loved her, which is a husband's first duty in marriage (see Ephesians 5:25; Colossians 3:19). Reciprocally, Rebekah comforted Isaac as the 'helper suitable for him', chosen by God for the covenant heir (see 2:18). In leaving her home and family she discovered her husband's love and became a member of the covenant community.

All love is costly. The joy and deep security of a loving marriage relationship is dependent on the responsibility of a life-long commitment, freely entered into and publicly witnessed. That is why God's guidance was (and still is) the crucial factor in the choice of a partner for those within the covenant family. Isaac and Rebekah must have needed to look back on the certainty of God's revealed plan for them many times during their marriage. Like Isaac's mother, his wife was barren. Again the fulfilment of the covenant promise seemed to lack its completion. Doubtless Isaac went through the same agonies of doubt and dismay as his father Abraham had done, but at least he could draw on his father's experience of God's faithfulness, and so he prayed (25:21). He and Rebekah had to wait twenty years before those prayers were answered with the birth of twins, Esau and Jacob. The line would continue, as God had promised, and in the next generation Jacob would become the father of twelve sons, who would themselves father the twelve tribes of Israel. Throughout the years the covenant people were learning Abraham's lesson, to believe the promises and obey the commands, to have faith in the God who is faithful, to discover and do his will.

The poet William Cowper (1731–1800) was to express those same truths thus centuries later:

> God moves in a mysterious way,
>     His wonders to perform;
> He plants His footsteps in the sea,
>     And rides upon the storm.
>
> Deep in unfathomable mines
>     of never-failing skill
> He treasures up His bright designs,
>     And works His sovereign will . . .
>
> His purposes will ripen fast,
>     Unfolding every hour;
> The bud may have a bitter taste,
>     But sweet will be the flower.
>
> Blind unbelief is sure to err,
>     And scan His work in vain;
> God is His own interpreter,
>     And He will make it plain.

# Epilogue

*Altogether, Abraham lived a hundred and seventy-five years. Then Abraham breathed his last and died at a good old age, an old man and full of years; and he was gathered to his people* (Genesis 25: 7–8).

So the patriarch's life came to its peaceful fulfilment and end. Abraham lived long enough to see his grandsons, Esau and Jacob, into their teens, and no doubt he loved to tell them the stories of his life's adventure of faith in God and fellowship with him. It was a hundred years after he had set out from Haran that he was buried by Isaac and Ishmael in the cave of Machpelah, near Mamre – a century of growing faith. Jacob was old enough to remember him well from his boyhood years, and to pass on the stories of grandfather Abraham to his twelve sons so that they might understand their unique position as Yahweh's covenant people. The heritage went with them when they followed Joseph into Egypt and it remained alive as the multiplying people of God waited in the land of bondage for four more centuries before the exodus deliverance and the eventual conquest and possession of the land of promise.

In that land Abraham was buried. When Sarah had died, over thirty years before his own death, he had had to acquire a family burial-place. So he had approached the Hittites to buy land for a burial site and eventually secured the cave of Machpelah, which was the property of Ephron the Hittite, and also the field where the cave was situated. Although Ephron appears to have been willing to give the land to Abraham, the patriarch insisted on paying the full market value, 400 shekels of silver. This was agreed and the field and cave became Abraham's legal property, as a burial site. Although a resident alien and a respected chief because of his wealth, Abraham had only restricted rights in Hittite society. Probably the desire to give him the land was a move to prevent him from gaining a stronger foothold by actually owning land, but he succeeded in purchasing it with a properly witnessed contract, and it was indeed the only piece of land Abraham ever owned. Here his sons buried the grand old man of faith, or at least his earthly remains, but what happened to Abraham?

The writer to the Hebrews in the New Testament tells us as he reviews the gallery of faith's heroes from Abel to Abraham. 'All these people were still living by faith when they died. They did not receive the things promised; they only saw them and welcomed them from a distance. And they admitted that they were aliens and strangers on earth. People who say such things show that they are looking for a country of their own. If they had been thinking of the country they had left, they would have had opportunity to return. Instead, they were longing for a better country – a heavenly one. Therefore God is not ashamed to be called their God, for he has prepared a city for them' (Hebrews 11:13–16).

Machpelah was not the end of the pilgrimage for Abraham. He believed God and it was counted to him as righteousness. So, in common with all who put their faith in God's grace revealed in Christ, Abraham was welcomed into the city prepared for him, the heavenly Jerusalem, into the very presence of God himself, where he is alive eternally. In confirmation of this fact we have even the words of the Lord Jesus Christ himself. In discussion with the Sadducees on the question of the resurrection (in which they did not believe), Jesus affirms, 'Even Moses showed that the dead rise, for he calls the Lord "the God of Abraham, and the God of Isaac, and the God of Jacob." He is not the God of the dead, but of the living, for to him all are alive' (Luke 20:37–38).

Just as none of the promises of God made in the covenant commitment to Abraham failed, so none of the promises of that eternal city, for which he looked, have failed. Abraham entered into eternal life through faith. The work of Christ, which was yet to take place in history, was as much the ground of his justification as it is of ours. So Jesus was able to affirm, again to his hostile Jewish critics, 'Your father Abraham rejoiced at the thought of seeing my day; he saw it and was glad' (John 8:56). What Abraham saw dimly as a future reality, we look back on as the historical foundation of our faith. But we are one with Abraham in that we too are those who believe and who have entered into the covenant grace of God through faith alone.

If that is our common call, then our lifestyle must be like his. We are called to an adventure of faith with the God who has proved himself to be utterly faithful. If we are Abraham's spiritual children, we must make sure that the family likeness is seen in the way we live. We too must be people who believe God. 'The Scripture foresaw that God would justify the Gentiles by faith, and announced the gospel in advance to Abraham: "All nations will be blessed through you." So those who have faith are blessed along with Abraham, the man of faith . . . There is neither Jew nor Greek, slave nor free, male nor female, for you are all one in Christ Jesus. If you belong to Christ, then you are Abraham's seed, and heirs according to the promise' (Galatians 3:8–9, 28–29).

## BIBLE BIOGRAPHIES

A new series of living and popular expositions
which bring out the personality, life,
importance and historical setting of Bible
characters, and what we can learn from them
today.

**ABRAHAM**
Believing God in an alien world
**David Jackman**

A vivid portrayal of Abraham's development as
a person of faith who plays his strategic part
in God's unfolding plan for human life and its
salvation.

*Pocketbook*      *160 pages*      *0–85110–498–3*

**JEREMIAH**
Speaking for God in a time of crisis
**David Day**

From the moment God calls Jeremiah, he
becomes God's hammer, breaking down the
pride and rebellion of his generation, a tool in
the hand of God who plans the transformation
of his people.

*Pocketbook*      *128 pages*      *0–85110–499–1*

Future titles to include:
  Elijah
  Nehemiah
  Joseph

**Inter-Varsity Press**